APPLAUSE FIRST FOLIO EDITIONS

The Lamentable Tragedie of Titus Andronicus

BY

William Shakespeare

PREPARED & ANNOTATED BY

NEIL FREEMAN

The Applause Shakespeare Library

Folio Texts

AN APPLAUSE ORIGINAL

The Lamentable Tragedie of Titus Andronicus

original concept devised by Neil Freeman

original research computer entry by Margaret McBride

original software programmes designed and developed by
James McBride and Terry Lim

Text layout designed and executed by Neil Freeman

Some elements of this text were privately published under the collective title of
The Freeman–Nichols Folio Scripts 1991–96

Copyright ° 1998, 2000 by Folio Scripts, Vancouver, Canada

ISBN: 1-55783-379-6

Library of Congress Cataloging-in-Publication Data

Library of Congress Catalog Card Number: 99-65416

British Library Cataloging-in-Publication Data

A catalogue record of this book is available from the British Library

APPLAUSE BOOKS

1841 Broadway Suite 1100
New York, NY 10023
Phone (212) 765-7880
Fax: (212) 765-7875

Combined Book Services Ltd.
Units I/K Paddock Wood Dist. Ctr.
Paddock Wood,
Tonbridge Kent TN12 6UU
Phone 0189 283-7171
Fax 0189 283-7272

Printed in Canada

CONTENTS

ACKNOWLEDGEMENTS

My grateful thanks to all who have helped in the growth and development of this work. Special thanks to Norman Welsh who first introduced me to the Folio Text, and to Tina Packer who (with Kristin Linklater and all the members of Shakespeare & Co.) allowed me to explore the texts on the rehearsal floor. To Jane Nichols for her enormous generosity in providing the funding which allowed the material to be computerised. To James and Margaret McBride and Terry Lim for their expertise, good humour and hard work. To the National Endowment for the Arts for their award of a Major Artist Fellowship and to York University for their award of the Joseph G. Green Fellowship. To actors, directors and dramaturgs at the Stratford Festival, Ontario; Toronto Free Theatre (that was); the Skylight Theatre, Toronto and Tamanhouse Theatre of Vancouver. To colleagues, friends and students at The University of British Columbia, Vancouver; York University, Toronto; Concordia University, Montreal; The National Theatre School of Canada in Montreal; Equity Showcase Theatre, Toronto; The Centre for Actors Study and Training (C.A.S.T.), Toronto; The National Voice Intensive at Simon Fraser University, Vancouver; Studio 58 of Langara College, Vancouver; Professional Workshops in the Arts, Vancouver; U.C.L.A., Los Angeles; Loyola Marymount, Los Angeles; San Jose State College, California; Long Beach State College, California; Brigham Young University, Utah, and Hawaii; Holy Cross College, Massachussetts; Guilford College, North Carolina. To Chairman John Wright and Associate Dean Don Paterson for their incredible personal support and encouragement. To Rachel Ditor and Tom Scholte for their timely research assistance. To Alan and Chris Baker, and Stephanie McWilliams for typographical advice. To Jay L. Halio, Hugh Richmond, and G.B. Shand for their critical input. To the overworked and underpaid proofreading teams of Ron Oten and Yuuattee Tanipersaud, Patrick Galligan and Leslie Barton, Janet Van De Graaff and Angela Dorhman (with input from Todd Sandomirsky, Bruce Alexander Pitkin, Catelyn Thornton and Michael Roberts). And above all to my wife Julie, for her patient encouragement, courteous advice, critical eye and long sufferance!

SPECIAL ACKNOWLEDGEMENTS

Paul Sugarman and Glenn Young of Applause Books; Houghton Mifflin Company for permission to quote from the line numbering system developed for *The Riverside Shakespeare*: Evans, Gwynne Blakemore, Harry Levin, Anne Barton, Herschel Baker, Frank Kermode, Hallet D. Smith, and Marie Edel, editors, *The Riverside Shakespeare*. Copyright © 1974 by Houghton Mifflin Company.

DEFINITIONS OF AND GUIDE TO PHOTOGRAPHIC COPIES OF THE EARLY TEXTS

(see Appendix A for a brief history of the First Folio, the Quartos,
and their uneasy relationship with modern texts)

A QUARTO (Q)

A single text, so called because of the book size resulting from a particular method of printing. Eighteen of Shakespeare's plays were published in this format by different publishers at various dates between 1594–1622 prior to the appearance of the 1623 Folio. Of the eighteen quarto texts, scholars suggest that fourteen have value as source texts. An extremely useful collection of them is to be found in Michael J. B. Allen and Kenneth Muir, eds., *Shakespeare's Plays in Quarto* (Berkeley: University of California Press, 1981).

THE FIRST FOLIO (F1)[1]

Thirty-six of Shakespeare's plays (excluding *Pericles* and *Two Noble Kinsmen,* in which he had a hand) appeared in one volume published in 1623. All books of this size were termed Folios, again because of the sheet size and printing method, hence this volume is referred to as the First Folio; two recent photographic editions of the work are:

Charlton Hinman, ed., *The Norton Facsimile (The First Folio of Shakespeare)* (1968; republished New York: W. W. Norton & Company, Inc., 1996).

Helge Kökeritz, ed., *Mr. William Shakespeare's Comedies, Histories & Tragedies* (New Haven: Yale University Press, 1954).

THE SECOND FOLIO (F2)

Scholars suggest that the Second Folio, dated 1632 but perhaps not published until 1640, has little authority, especially since it created hundreds of new problematical readings of its own. Nevertheless, more than eight hundred modern text readings can be attributed to it. The most recent reproduction is D. S. Brewer, ed., *Mr.*

---

[1] For a full overview of the First Folio see the monumental two-volume work: Charlton Hinman, *The Printing and Proof Reading of the First Folio of Shakespeare* (2 volumes) (Oxford: Clarendon Press, 1963) and W. W. Greg, *The Editorial Problem in Shakespeare: a Survey of the Foundations of the Text,* 3rd. ed. (Oxford: Clarendon Press, 1954); for a brief summary, see the forty-six page publication from Peter W. M. Blayney, *The First Folio of Shakespeare* (Washington, DC: Folger Library Publications, 1991).

William Shakespeare's Comedies, Histories & Tragedies, the Second Folio Reproduced in Facsimile (Dover, NH: Boydell & Brewer Ltd., 1985).

The Third Folio (1664) and the Fourth Folio (1685) have even less authority, and are rarely consulted except in cases of extreme difficulty.

THE THIRD FOLIO (F3)

The Third Folio, carefully proofed (though apparently not against the previous edition) takes great pains to correct anomalies in punctuation ending speeches and in expanding abbreviations. It also introduced seven new plays supposedly written by Shakespeare, only one of which, *Pericles*, has been established as such. The most recent reproduction is D. S. Brewer, ed., *Mr. William Shakespeare's Comedies, Histories & Tragedies, the Third Folio Reproduced in Facsimile* (Dover, NH: Boydell & Brewer Ltd., 1985).

THE FOURTH FOLIO (F4)

Paradoxically, while the Fourth Folio was the most carefully edited of all, its concentration on grammatical clarity and ease of comprehension by its readers at the expense of faithful reproduction of F1 renders it the least useful for those interested in the setting down on paper of Elizabethan theatre texts. The most recent reproduction is D. S. Brewer, ed., *Mr. William Shakespeare's Comedies, Histories & Tragedies, the Fourth Folio Reproduced in Facsimile* (Dover, NH: Boydell & Brewer Ltd., 1985).

WELCOME TO THESE SCRIPTS

These scripts are designed to do three things:

1. show the reader what the First Folio (often referred to as F1) set down on paper, rather than what modern editions think ought to have been set down

2. provide both reader and theatre practitioner an easy journey through some of the information the original readers might have garnered from F1 and other contemporary scripts which is still relevant today

3. provide a simple way for readers to see not only where modern texts alter the First Folio, and how, but also allow readers to explore both First Folio and modern versions of the disputed passage without having to turn to an Appendix or a different text

all this, hopefully without interfering with the action of the play.

What the First Folio sets on paper will be the basis for what you see. In the body of the play-text that follows, the words (including spellings and capitalisations), the punctuation (no matter how ungrammatical), the structure of the lines (including those moments of peculiar verse or unusual prose), the stage directions, the act and scene divisions, and (for the most part) the prefixes used for each character will be as set in the First Folio.

In addition, new, on page, visual symbols specially devised for these texts will help point out both the major stepping stones in the Elizabethan debate/rhetorical process contained in the plays (a fundamental part of understanding both the inner nature of each character as well as the emotional clashes between them), and where and how (and sometimes why) modern texts have altered the First Folio information. And, unlike any other script, opposite each page of text will be a blank page where readers can make their own notes and commentary.

However, there will be the rare occasion when these texts do not exactly follow the First Folio.

Sometimes F1's **words or phrases** are meaningless; for example, the lovely misprinting of 'which' in *Twelfth Night* as 'wh?ch', or in *Romeo and Juliet* the type-setting corruptions of 'speeh' for 'speech' and the running of the two words 'not away' as 'notaway'. If there are no alternative contemporary texts (a Quarto version of the play) or if no modification was made by any of the later Folios (The Second Folio of 1632, The Third Folio of 1664, or The Fourth Folio of 1685, termed F2, F3, and F4 respectively) then the F1 printing will be set as is, no matter how peculiar, and the modern correction footnoted. However, if a more appropriate alternative is available in a Quarto (often referred to as Q) or F2, F3, or F4, that 'correction' will be set directly into the text, replacing the F1 reading, and footnoted accordingly, as in the case of 'wh?ch', 'speeh', and 'notaway'.

The only time F1's **punctuation** will be altered is when the original setting is so blurred that an accurate deciphering of what F1 set cannot be determined. In such cases, alternative punctuation from F2–4 or Q will be set and a footnote will explain why.

The only time F1's **line structure** will not be followed is when at the end of a very long line, the final word or part of the word cannot fit onto the single line, nor be set as a new line in F1 because of the text that follows and is therefore set above or below the original line at the right hand side of the column. In such rare cases these texts will complete the line as a single line, and mark it with a † to show the change from F1. In all other cases, even when in prose F1 is forced to split the final word of a speech in half, and set only a few letters of it on a new line—for example in *Henry the Fifth*, Pistoll's name is split as 'Pi' on one line and 'stoll' (as the last part of the speech) on the next—these texts will show F1 exactly as set.

Some liberties have to be taken with the **prefixes** (the names used at the beginning of speeches to show the reader which character is now speaking), for Ff (all the Folios) and Qq (all the Quartos) are not always consistent. Sometimes slightly different abbreviations are used for the same character—in *The Tempest*, King Alonso is variously referred to as 'Al.', 'Alo.', 'Alon.', and 'Alonso'. Sometimes the same abbreviation is used for two different characters—in *A Midsummer Nights Dream* the characters Quince, the 'director' and author of the Mechanicals play, and Titania, Queen of the fairies, are given the same abbreviation 'Qu.'. While in this play common sense can distinguish what is intended, the confusions in *Julius Caesar* between Lucius and Lucullus, each referred to sometimes as 'Luc.', and in *The Comedy of Errors,* where the twin brothers Antipholus are both abbreviated to 'Antiph.', cannot be so easily sorted out. Thus, whereas F1 will show a variety of abbreviated prefixes, these texts will usually choose just one complete name per character and stay with it throughout.

However, there are certain cases where one full name will not suffice. Sometimes F1 will change the prefix for a single character from scene to scene, the change usually reflecting the character's new function or status. Thus in *The Comedy of Errors,* as a drinking companion of the local Antipholus, the goldsmith Angelo is referred to by his given name 'Ang.', but once business matters go awry he very quickly becomes a businessman, referred to as 'Gold'. Similar changes affect most of the characters in *A Midsummer Nights Dream,* and a complex example can be found in *Romeo and Juliet.* While modern texts give Juliet's mother the single prefix Lady Capulet throughout (incorrectly since neither she nor Capulet are named as aristocrats anywhere in the play) both Ff and Qq refer to her in a wonderful character-revealing multiplicity of ways—Mother, Capulet Wife, Lady, and Old Lady—a splendid gift for actress, director, designer, and reader alike.

Surprisingly, no modern text ever sets any of these variations. Believing such changes integral to the development of the characters so affected, these texts will. In such cases, each time the character's prefix changes the new prefix will be set, and a small notation alongside the prefix (either by reference to the old name, or by adding the symbol •) will remind the reader to whom it refers.

Also, some alterations will be made to F1's **stage directions,** not to the words themselves or when they occur, but to the way they are going to be presented visually. Scholars agree F1 contains two different types of stage direction: those that came in the original manuscript from which the Playhouse copy of the play was made, and a second set that were added in for theatrical clarification by the Playhouse. The scholars conjecture that the literary or manuscript directions, presumably from Shakespeare, mainly dealing with entries and key actions such as battles, are those that F1 sets centred on a separate line, while the additional Playhouse directions, usually dealing with offstage sounds, music, and exits, are those F1 sets alongside the spoken dialogue, usually flush against the right hand side of the column. In performance terms there seems to be a useful distinction between the two, though this is only a rule of thumb. The centred manuscript (Shakespearean?) directions tend to stop or change the action of the play, that is, the scene is affected by the action the direction demands, whereas the Playhouse directions (to the side of the text) serve to underscore what is already taking place. (If a word is needed to distinguish the two, the centred directions can be called 'action' directions, because they are events in and of themselves, while the side-set directions could be called 'supportive' or 'continuous' since they tend not to distract from the current onstage action.)

Since F1 seems to visually distinguish between the two types (setting them on different parts of the page) and there seems to be a logical theatrical differentiation as to both the source and function of each, it seems only appropriate that these scripts also mark the difference between them. Both Ff and Qq's side-set directions are often difficult to decipher while reading the text: sometimes they are set so close to the spoken text they get muddled up with it, despite the different typeface, and oftentimes have to be abbreviated to fit in. These are drawbacks shared by most modern texts. Thus these texts will distinguish them in a slightly different way (see p. xxvi below).

Finally, there will be two occasional alterations to Ff's **fonts.** F1 used **italics** for a large number of different purposes, sometimes creating confusion on the page. What these texts will keep as italics are letters, poems, songs, and the use of foreign languages. What they will not set in italics are real names, prefixes, and stage directions. Also at the top of each play, and sometimes at the beginning of a letter or poem, F1 would set a large wonderfully **decorative opening letter,** with the second letter of the word being capitalised, the style tying in with the borders that surrounded the opening and closing of each play. Since these texts will not be reproducing the decorative borders, the decorative letters won't be set either.

MAKING FULL USE OF THESE TEXTS

WHAT MODERN CHANGES WILL BE SHOWN

WORDS AND PHRASES

Modern texts often tidy up F1's words and phrases. Real names, both of people and places, and foreign languages are often reworked for modern understanding; for example, the French town often set in F1 as 'Callice' is usually reset as 'Calais'. Modern texts 'correct' the occasional Elizabethan practice of setting a singular noun with plural verb (and vice versa), as well as the infrequent use of the past tense of a verb to describe a current situation. These texts will set the F1 reading, and footnote the modern corrections whenever they occur.

More problematical are the possibilities of choice, especially when a Q and F version of the same play show a different reading for the same line and either choice is valid—even more so when both versions are offered by different modern texts. Juliet's 'When I shall die,/Take him and cut him out in little starres' offered by Ff/Q1-3 being offset by Q4's 'When he shall die...' is a case in point. Again, these texts will set the F1 reading, and footnote the alternatives.

LINE STRUCTURE CHANGES RELATED TO PROBLEMS OF 'CASTING-OFF'

The First Folio was usually prepared in blocks of twelve pages at a time. Six pairs of pages would be prepared, working both forward and backward simultaneously. Thus from the centre of any twelve-page block, pages six and seven were set first, then five and eight, then four and nine, then three and ten, then two and eleven, and finally one and twelve. This meant each compositor had to work out very carefully how much copy would fit not only each sheet, but also how much would be needed overall to reach the outer edges of pages one and twelve to match it to the previously set text, (prior to page one) or about to be set text (after page twelve). Naturally the calculations weren't always accurate. Sometimes there was too little text left for too great a space: in such cases, if the manuscript were set as it should have been, a great deal of empty paper would be left free, a condition often described as 'white' space. Sometimes too much text remained for too small a space, and if the manuscript were to be set according to its normal layout, every available inch would be taken up with type (and even then the text might not fit), a condition that could be described as 'crammed space'.

Essentially, this created a huge design problem, and most commentators suggest when it arose the printing house policy was to sacrifice textual accuracy to neatness of design. Thus, so the argument goes, in the case of white space, extra lines of type would have to be created where (presumably) none originally existed. *Hamlet* provides an excellent example with the Polonius speech 'Indeed that's out of the air' starting at line 78 of what most modern texts term Act Two Scene 2. Q2 sets the four-line speech as prose, and most modern texts follow suit. However, F1, faced with a potentially huge white space problem at the bottom of the right hand column of p. 261 in the Tragedy section, resets the speech as eleven lines of very irregular verse! In the case of crammed space, five lines of verse might suddenly become three lines of prose, or in one very severe case of overcrowding in *Henry The Fourth Part Two*, words, phrases, and even half lines of text might be omitted to reduce the text sufficiently.

When such cases occur, this text will set F1 as shown, and the modern texts' suggested alternatives will be footnoted and discussed.

LINE STRUCTURE CHANGES NOT RELATED TO PROBLEMS OF 'CASTING-OFF'

In addition, modern texts regularly make changes to F1's line structure which are not related to 'white' or 'crammed' space, often to the detriment of both character and scene. Two major reasons are offered for the changes.

First, either (a few) prose lines suddenly appear in what essentially is a verse scene (or a few verse lines in a sea of prose) and the modern texts, feeling the scene should be standardised, restructure the offending lines accordingly. *The Tempest* is atrociously served this way[2], for where F1, the only source text, shows the conspirators Caliban, Stephano, and, very occasionally, Trinculo, speaking verse as well as prose even within the same speech (a sure sign of personal striving and inner disturbance) most modern texts readjust the lines to show only Caliban speaking verse (dignifying him more than he deserves) and Stephano and Trinculo only speaking prose (thus robbing them of their dangerous flights of fancy).

Second, some Ff verse lines appear so appallingly defective in terms of their rhythm and length that modern texts feel it necessary to make a few 'readjustments' of the lines around them to bring the offending lines back to a coherent, rhythmic whole. Many of the later plays are abominably served in this regard: in *Macbeth*, for example, over a hundred F1 passages involving more than 200 lines (90 percent of which were set by the usually reliable compositor A) have been altered by most modern texts. Most of these changes concentrate on regularising moments where a character is under tremendous upheaval and hardly likely to be speaking pure formal verse at that particular moment!

These changes come about through a mistaken application of modern grammat-

---

[2] Commentators suggest the copy play used for setting F1, coming from Stratford as it did, and thus unsupervised by Shakespeare in the Playhouse preparation of the document, prepared by Ralph Crane, was at times defective, especially in distinguishing clearly between verse and prose: this is why most modern texts do not follow F1's choices in these dubious passages: readers are invited to explore *The Tempest* within this series, especially the footnotes, as a theatrical vindication of the original F1 setting

ical considerations to texts that were originally prepared not according to grammar but rhetoric. One of rhetoric's many strengths is that it can show not only when characters are in self-control but also when they are not. In a rhetorically set passage, the splutters of a person going through an emotional breakdown, as with Othello, can be shown almost verbatim, with peculiar punctuations, spellings, breaks, and all. If the same passage were to be set grammatically it would be very difficult to show the same degree of personal disintegration on the printed page.[3] F1's occasional weird shifts between verse and prose and back again, together with the moments of extreme linear breakdown, are the equivalents of human emotional breakdown, and once the anomalies of Elizabethan script preparation are accounted for,[4] the rhetorical breakdowns on F1's printed page are clear indications of a character's disintegration within the play. When modern texts tidy up such blemishes grammatically they unwittingly remove essential theatrical and/or character clues for reader and theatre person alike.

In these texts, F1's line structure will be set as is, and all such modern alterations (prose to verse, verse to prose, regularisation of originally unmetrical lines) will be shown. The small symbol ° will be added to show where modern texts suggest a line should end rather than where F1 shows it does. A thin vertical line will be set to the left alongside any text where the modern texts have converted F1's prose to verse, or vice versa. The more large-scale of these changes will be boxed for quicker reader recognition. Most of these changes will be footnoted in the text where they occur, and a comparison of the two different versions of the text and what each could signify theatrically will be offered. For examples of both, see p. xxiii below.

THE SPECIAL PROBLEMS AFFECTING WHAT ARE KNOWN AS 'SHARED' OR 'SPLIT' VERSE LINES

A definition, and their importance to the Shakespeare texts

Essentially, split lines are short lines of verse which, when placed together, form the equivalent of a full verse line. Most commentators suggest they are very useful in speeding the play along, for the second character (whose line attaches on to the end of the first short line) is expected to use the end of the first character's line as a

---

[3] For a full discussion of this, readers are directed to Neil Freeman, *Shakespeare's First Texts* (Vancouver: Folio Scripts, 1994).

[4] Readers are referred to an excellent chapter by Gary Taylor which analyses the whole background, conjectured and known, concerning the preparation of the first scripts. He points out the pitfalls of assuming the early texts as sole authority for all things Shakespearean: he examines the conjectured movement of the scripts from Shakespeare's pen to printed edition, and carefully examples the changes and alterations that could occur, (most notably at the hands of the manuscript copyists), as well as the interferences and revampings of the Playhouse, plus the effects of the first typesetters' personal habits and carelessness. Stanley Wells and Gary Taylor, *William Shakespeare: A Textual Companion* (Oxford: Clarendon Press, 1987), 1–68.

springboard and jump in with an immediate reply, enhancing the quickness of the debate. Thus in *Measure for Measure*, Act Two Scene 2, modern ll. 8–10, the Provost, trying to delay Claudio's execution, has asked Angelo whether Claudio has to die the following day: Angelo's questioning affirmation ends with a very pointed short line, followed immediately by a short line opening from the Provost.

Angelo	Did I not tell thee yea? hadst thou not order?
	Why do'st thou aske againe?
Provost	Lest I might be too rash:
	Under your good correction, I have seene
	When after execution...

If the Provost replies immediately after, or just as, Angelo finishes, an explosive dramatic tension is created. Allowing a minor delay before reply, as many actors do, will reduce the impact of the moment, and create a hesitation where one probably does not exist.

The occasional problem

So far so good. But the problems start when more than two short lines follow each other. If there are three short lines in succession, which should be joined, #1 and #2, or #2 and #3? Later in the same scene, Claudio's sister Isabella has, at the insistence of Claudio's friend Lucio, come to plead with Angelo for her brother's life. In Lucio's eyes she is giving up too easily, hence the following (modern ll. 45–49):

Lucio	You are too cold: if you should need a pin,
	You could not with more tame a tongue desire it:
	To him, I say.
Isabella	Must he needs die?
Angelo	Maiden, no remedie?

And here it seems fairly obvious Isabella and Angelo's lines should join together, thus allowing a wonderful dramatic pause following Lucio's urging before Isabella plucks up enough courage to try. Most modern texts set the lines accordingly, with Lucio's the short odd line out.

But what about the three lines contained in the exchange that follows almost straightaway?

Isabella	But you might doe't & do the world no wrong
	If so your heart were touch'd with that remorse,
	As mine is to him?
Angelo	Hee's sentenc'd, tis too late.
Lucio	You are too cold.
Isabella	Too late? why no: I that doe speak a word

> May call it againe: well, beleeve this
>
> (modern line numbering 53–56)

Does Angelo's 'Hee's sentenc'd...' spring off Isabella's line, leaving Isabella speechless and turning to go before Lucio urges her on again? Or does Angelo pause (to frame a reply?) before speaking, leaving Lucio to quickly jump in quietly giving Isabella no time to back off? Either choice is possible, and dramatically valid. And readers should be allowed to make their own choice, which automatically means each reader should able to see the possibility of such choices when they occur.

The problem magnified by the way modern texts set split/shared lines

However, because of a peculiarity faced by the modern texts not shared by Ff/Qq, modern texts rarely show such possibilities to their readers but make the choice for them. The peculiarity comes about from a change in text layout initiated in the eighteenth century.

Ff/Qq always set short lines directly under one another, as shown in the examples above. In 1778 George Steevens, a highly respected editor, started to show split lines a new way, by advancing the second split line to just beyond where the first split line finishes, viz.

Angelo	Did I not tell thee yea? hadst thou not order?
	Why do'st thou aske againe?
Provost	Lest I might be too rash:
	Under your good correction, I have seene
	When after execution...

Since that date all editions of Shakespeare have followed this practice, which is fine as long as there are only two short lines, but when three follow each other, a choice has to be made. Thus the second Isabella/Angelo/Lucio sequence could be set as either

Isabella	But you might doe't & do the world no wrong
	If so your heart were touch'd with that remorse,
	As mine is to him?
Angelo	Hee's sentenc'd, tis too late.
Lucio	You are too cold.
Isabella	Too late? why no: I that doe speak a word
	May call it againe: well, beleeve this...

(the usual modern choice), or

Isabella	But you might doe't & do the world no wrong
	If so your heart were touch'd with that remorse,
	As mine is to him?

Angelo	Hee's sentenc'd, tis too late.
Lucio	You are too cold.
Isabella	Too late? why no: I that doe speak a word
	May call it againe: well, beleeve this...

This modern typesetting convention has robbed the reader of a very important moment of choice. Indeed, at the beginning of the twentieth century, Richard Flatter[5] suggested that what modern commentators consider to be split lines may not be split lines at all. He offers two other suggestions: pauses and hesitations could exist between each line, or the lines could in fact be spoken one on top of another, a very important consideration for the crowd responses to Anthony in the funeral scene of *Julius Caesar*. Either way, the universally adopted Steevens layout precludes the reader/theatre practitioner from even seeing such possibilities.

These texts will show the F1 layout as is, and will indicate via footnote when a choice is possible (in the case of three short lines, or more, in succession) and by the symbol } when the possibility of springboarding exists. Thus the Folio Texts would show the first Angelo/Provost example as:

Angelo	Did I not tell thee yea? hadst thou not order?
	Why do'st thou aske againe?
	}
Provost	Lest I might be too rash:
	Under your good correction, I have seene
	When after execution...

In nearly all cases the } shows where most modern texts insist on setting a shared split line. However, readers are cautioned that in many of the later plays, the single line so created is much longer than pentameter, and often very a-rhythmic. In such cases the lines could have great value as originally set (two separate short lines), especially when a key debate is in process (for example, *Measure for Measure*, *The Tragedie of Cymbeline*, *Othello*, and *The Winters Tale*).

THE UNUSUAL SINGLE SPLIT LINE (PLEASE SEE 'A CAVEAT', P. XXXVIII)

So far the discussion has centred on short lines shared by two or more characters. Ff/Qq offer another complication rarely, if ever, accepted by most modern texts. Quite often, and not because of white space, a single character will be given two consecutive short lines within a single speech. *Romeo and Juliet* is chock full of this device: in the famous balcony scene (modern texts numbering 2.2.62–3) Juliet asks Romeo

How cam'st thou hither.

---

[5]   Richard Flatter, *Shakespeare's Producing Hand* (London: Heinemann, 1948, reprint).

> Tell me, and wherefore?
> The Orchard walls are high, and hard to climbe

The first two lines (five syllables each) suggest a minute pause between them as Juliet hesitates before asking the all important second line (with its key second part 'and wherefore'). Since Qq rarely set such 'single split lines' most modern texts refuse to set any of them, but combine them:

> How cams't thou hither. Tell me and wherefore?

This basically F1 device is set by all the compositors and followed by all other Folios. This text will follow suit, highlighting them with the symbol → for quick recognition, viz.:

> How cam'st thou hither. →
> Tell me, and wherefore?
> The Orchard walls are high, and hard to climbe

SENTENCE AND PUNCTUATION STRUCTURES

A CHARACTER'S THOUGHTFUL & EMOTIONAL JOURNEY

A quick comparison between these texts and both the Ff/Qq's and the modern texts will reveal two key differences in the layout of the dialogue on the printed page — the bolding of major punctuation, and the single line dropping of text whenever a new sentence begins.

The underlying principle behind these texts is that since the handwritten documents from which they stem were originally intended for the actor and Playhouse, in addition to their poetical values, the Ff/Qq scripts represent a theatrical process. Even if the scripts are being read just for pleasure, at the back of the reader's mind should be the notion of characters on a stage and actors acting (and the word 'process' rather than 'practice' is deliberate, with process suggesting a progression, development, or journey).

The late Jean-Louis Barrault gave a wonderful definition of acting, and of this journey, suggesting an actor's job was to strive to remain in 'the ever-changing present'. If something happens onstage (an entry, an exit, a verbal acceptance or denial of what the actor's character has suggested), the 'present' has changed, and the character must readjust accordingly. Just as onstage, the actor should be prepared for the character to re-adjust, and in rehearsal should be examining how and why it does, so should the reader in the library, armchair, or classroom.

In many ways, the key to Shakespeare is discovering how each character's mind works; perceiving the emotions and intellects as they act and react helps the reader understand from where the poetical imagination and utterance stem.

Certain elements of each character's emotional and intellectual journey, and where it changes, are encoded into the sentence structure of Ff/Qq.

Elizabethan education prepared any schooled individual (via the 'petty school' and the private tutor) for the all important and essential daily rough and tumble of argument and debate. Children were trained not only how to frame an argument so as to win it hands down, but also how to make it entertaining so as to enthrall the neutral listener.

The overall training, known as 'rhetoric', essentially allowed intellect and emotion to exist side by side, encouraging the intellect to keep the emotion in check. The idea was not to deny the emotions, but ensure they didn't swamp the 'divinity' of reason, the only thing separating man from beast. While the initial training was mainly vocal, any written matter of the period automatically reflected the ebb and flow of debate. What was set on the printed page was not grammar, but a representation of the rhetorical process.

DROPPING A LINE TO ILLUSTRATE F1'S SENTENCE STRUCTURE

Put at its simplest, in any document of the period, each sentence would represent a new intellectual and emotional stage of a rhetorical argument. When this stage of the argument was completed, a period would be set (occasionally a question mark or, much more rarely, an exclamation mark—both followed by a capital letter) signifying the end of that stage of the argument, and the beginning of the next.

Thus in the First Folio, the identification of each new sentence is an automatic (and for us, four hundred years later, a wonderful) aid to understanding how a character is reacting to and dealing with Barrault's ever-changing present.

To help the reader quickly spot the new steppingstone in an argument, and thus the point of transition, these texts highlight where one sentence ends and the new one begins by simply dropping a line whenever a new sentence starts. Thus the reader has a visual reminder that the character is making a transition to deal with a change in the current circumstances of the scene (or in the process of self-discovery in the case of soliloquies).

This device has several advantages. The reader can instantly see where the next step in the argument begins. The patterns so created on the page can quickly illuminate whenever a contrast between characters' thought patterns occurs. (Sometimes the sentences are short and precise, suggesting the character is moving quickly from one idea to the next. Sometimes the sentences are very long, suggesting the character is undergoing a very convoluted process. Sometimes the sentences contain nothing but facts, suggesting the character has no time to entertain; sometimes they are filled with high-flown imagery, perhaps suggesting the character is trying to mask a very weak argument with verbal flummery.) The patterns can also show when a character's style changes within itself, say from long and convoluted to short and precise, or vice versa. It can also immediately pinpoint when a character is in trouble and not arguing coherently or logically, something modern texts often alter out of grammatical necessity.

With patience, all this could be gleaned from the modern texts (in as far as they set the Ff sentence structure, which they often don't) and from a photostat of the First Folio, by paying special attention to where the periods are set. But there is one extra very special advantage to this new device of dropping a line: this has to do once more with the Elizabethan method of setting down spoken argument on paper, especially when the character speaking is not in the best of all possible worlds.

If an Elizabethan person/character is arguing well, neatly, cleanly, tidily, then a printed representation of that argument would also be clean, neat, and tidy—to modern eyes it would be grammatically acceptable. If the same character is emotionally upset, or incapable of making a clear and tidy argument, then the on-paper representation would be muddy and untidy—to modern eyes totally ungrammatical and often not acceptable. By slightly isolating each sentence these texts very quickly allow the reader to spot when a sentence's construction is not all that it should be, say in the middle of Viola's so-called ring speech in *Twelfth Night* (Act Two Scene 2), or Helena's declaration of love for Bertram in *All's Well That Ends Well* (Act One Scene 3), or the amazing opening to *As You Like It,* where Orlando's opening litany of complaint against his brother starts with a single sentence twenty lines long.

This is especially relevant when a surprising modern editorial practice is accounted for. Very often the Ff sentence structures are markedly altered by modern texts, especially when the Ff sentences do not seem 'grammatical'—thus Orlando's twenty-line monster is split into six separate, grammatically correct sentences by all modern texts. And then there is the case of Shylock in *The Merchant of Venice,* a Jewish man being goaded and tormented beyond belief by the very Christians who helped his daughter elope with a Christian, taking a large part of Shylock's fortune with her. A sentence comparison of the famous Act Three Scene 1 speech culminating in 'Hath not a Jew eyes?' is very instructive. All modern texts set the speech as between fifteen and seventeen sentences in length: whatever the pain, anger, and personal passion, the modern texts encourage dignity and self-control, a rational Shylock. But this is a Shylock completely foreign to both Q1 and Ff. Q1 show the same speech as only four sentences long, Ff five—a veritable onflow of intellect and passion all mixed together, all unstoppable for the longest period of time—a totally different being from that shown by the modern texts. What is more, this is a totally different Shylock from the one seen earlier in the Ff/Q1 version of the play, where, even in the extremes of discomfort with the old enemy Anthonio, his sentence structures are rhetorically balanced and still grammatical to modern eyes.

Here, with Shylock, there are at least three benefits to dropping the sentence: the unusualness of the speech is immediately spotted; the change in style between this and any of his previous speeches can be quickly seen; and, above all, the moment where the speech moves from a long unchecked outpouring to a quick series of brief, dangerously rational sentences can be quickly identified. And these advantages will be seen in such changed sentence circumstances in any play in any of these texts.

THE HIGHLIGHTING OF THE MAJOR PUNCTUATION IN THESE TEXTS

A second key element of rhetoric encoded into the Ff/Qq texts clearly shows the characters' mind in action. The encoding lies in the remaining punctuation which, unlike much modern punctuation, serves a double function, one dealing with the formation of the thought, the other with the speaking of it.

Apart from the period, dealt with already, essentially there are two sets of punctuation to consider, minor and major, each with their own very specific functions.

Shakespearean characters reflect the mode of thinking of their time. Elizabethans were trained to constantly add to or modify thoughts. They added a thought to expand the one already made. They denied the first thought so as to set up alternatives. They elaborated a thought so as to clarify what has already been said. They suddenly moved into splendid puns or non-sequiturs (emotional, logical, or both) because they had been immediately stimulated by what they or others had just said. The **minor punctuation** (essentially the comma [,] the parenthesis or bracket [( )], and the dash) reflects all this.

In establishing thought processes for each character, minor punctuation shows every new nuance of thought: every tiny punctuation in this category helps establish the deftness and dance of each character's mind. In *As You Like It* (Act Three Scene 2, modern line numbering 400–402) the Ff setting of Rosalind's playing with her beloved Orlando has a wonderful coltish exuberance as she runs rings round his protestations of love:

> Love is meerely a madnesse, and I tel you,
> deserves as well a darke house,* and a whip,* as madmen do:

Her mind is adding extra thoughts as she goes: the Ff commas are as much part of her spirit and character as the words are—though most modern texts create a much more direct essayist, preaching what she already knows, by removing the two Ff commas marked *.[6]

A similar situation exists with Macbeth, facing Duncan whom he must kill if he is

---

[6] Unfortunately, many modern texts eradicate the F and Q minor punctuation arguing the need for light (or infrequent) punctuation to preserve the speed of speech. This is not necessarily helpful, since what it removes is just a new thought marker, not an automatic indication to pause: too often the result is that what the first texts offer a character as a series of closely-worked out dancing thought-patterns (building one quick thought—as marked by a comma—on top of another) is turned into a series of much longer phrases: often, involved and reactive busy minds are artificially turned into (at best) eloquent ones, suddenly capable of perfect and lengthy rationality where the situation does not warrant such a reaction, or (at worst) vapid ones, speaking an almost preconceived essay of commentary or artificial sentimentality.

to become king (Act One Scene 4, modern line numbering 22–27). Ff show a
Macbeth almost swamped with extra thoughts as he assures Duncan

> The service,* and the loyaltie I owe,
> In doing it,* payes it selfe.
> Your highnesse part,* is to receive our Duties,
> And our Duties are to your Throne,* and State,
> Children,* and Servants; which doe but what they should,*
> By doing every thing safe toward your Love
> And Honour.

The heavy use of minor punctuation — especially when compared with most
modern texts which remove the commas marked *, leaving Macbeth with just six
thoughts compared to Ff's twelve — clearly shows a man ill at ease and/or working
too hard to say the right thing. Again the punctuation helps create an understanding
of the character.

However, while the minor punctuation is extremely important in the discovery
process of reading and/or rehearsal, paradoxically, it mustn't become too dominant.
From the performance/speaking viewpoint, to pause at each comma would be tan-
tamount to disaster. There would be an enormous dampening effect if reader/actor
were to pause at every single piece of punctuation: the poetry would be destroyed
and the event would become interminable.

In many ways, minor punctuation is the Victorian child of Shakespearean texts,
it must be seen but not heard. (In speaking the text, the new thought the minor
punctuation represents can be added without pausing: a change in timbre, rhythm,
or pitch — in acting terms, occurring naturally with changes in intention — will do the
trick.)

But once thoughts have been discovered, they have to be organised into some
form of coherent whole. If the period shows the end of one world and the start of
the new, and if the comma marks a series of small, ever-changing, ever-evolving
thoughts within each world, occasionally there must be pause for reflection somewhere in the helter-skelter of tumbling new ideas. This is the **major punctuation's**
strength; major punctuation consisting of the semicolon [;], and the colon [:].

Major punctuation marks the gathering together of a series of small thoughts
within an overall idea before moving onto something new. If a room full of Rodin
sculptures were analogous to an Elizabethan scene or act, each individual piece of
sculpture would be a speech, the torso or back or each major limb a separate sentence. Each collective body part (a hand, the wrist, the forearm, the upper arm)
would be a series of small thoughts bounded by major punctuation, each smaller
item within that part (a finger, a fingernail, a knuckle) a single small thought separated by commas. In describing the sculpture to a friend one might move from the
smaller details (the knuckle) to the larger (the hand) to another larger (the wrist)

then another (the forearm) and so on to the whole limb. Unless the speaker is emotionally moved by the recollection, some pauses would be essential, certainly after finishing the whole description of the arm (the sentence), and probably after each major collective of the hand, the wrist, etc. (as marked by the major punctuation), but not after every small bit.

As a rule of thumb, and simply stated, the colon and semicolon mark both a thinking and a speaking pause. The vital difference between major and minor punctuation, whether in the silent reading of the text or the performing of it aloud, is you need not pause at the comma, bracket, or dash; you probably should at the colon, semicolon, and period.

Why the Major Punctuation is Bolded in These Texts.

In speaking the text or reading it, the minor punctuation indicates the need to key onto the new thought without necessarily requiring a pause. In so doing, the inherent rhythms of speech, scene, and play can clip along at the rate suggested by the Prologue in *Romeo and Juliet,* 'the two hours traffic of the stage', until a pause is absolutely necessary. Leave the commas alone, and the necessary pauses will make themselves known.

The 'major' punctuation then comes into its own, demanding double attention as both a thinking and speaking device. This is why it is bolded, to highlight it for the reader's easier access. The reader can still use all the punctuation when desired, working through the speech thought by thought, taking into account both major and minor punctuation as normal. Then, when needed, the bolding of the major punctuation will allow the reader easy access for marking where the speech, scene, or play needs to be broken down into its larger thinking/speaking (and even breathing) units without affecting its overall flow.

The Blank Pages Within the Text

In each text within this series, once readers reach the play itself they will find that with each pair of pages the dialogue is printed on the right-hand page only. The left-hand page has been deliberately left blank so that readers, actors, directors, stage managers, teachers, etc. have ample space for whatever notes and text emendations they may wish to add.

PRACTICAL ON-PAGE HELP FOR THE READER

THE VISUAL SYMBOLS HIGHLIGHTING MODERN ALTERATIONS

THE BOX

This surrounds a passage where the modern texts have made whole-scale alterations to the Ff text. Each boxed section will be footnoted, and the changes analysed at the bottom of the page.

THE FOOTNOTES

With many modern texts the footnotes are not easily accessible. Often no indication is given within the text itself where the problem/choice/correction exists. Readers are forced into a rather cumbersome four-step process. First, they have to search through the bottom of the page where the footnotes are crammed together, often in very small print, to find a line number where an alteration has been made. Then they must read the note to find out what has been altered. Then they must go back to the text and search the side of the page to find the corresponding line number. Having done all this, finally they can search the line to find the word or phrase that has been changed (sometimes complicated by the fact the word in question is set twice in different parts of the line).

These texts will provide a reference marker within the text itself, directly alongside the word or phrase that is in question. This guides the reader directly to the corresponding number in the footnote section of the bottom of each page, to the alteration under discussion — hopefully a much quicker and more immediate process.

In addition, since there are anywhere between 300 and 1,100 footnotes in any one of these texts, a tool is offered to help the reader find only those notes they require, when they require them. In the footnote section, prior to the number that matches the footnote marker in the text, a letter or combination of letters will be set as a code. The letter 'W', for example, shows that the accompanying footnote refers to word substitutions offered by modern texts; the letters 'SD' refer to an added or altered stage direction; the letters 'LS' show the footnote deals with a passage where the modern texts have completely altered the line-structure that F1 set. This enables readers to be selective when they want to examine only certain changes, for they can quickly skim through the body of footnotes until they find the code they want, perhaps those dealing with changes in prefixes (the code 'P') or when modern alterations have been swapping lines from verse to prose or vice versa (the code 'VP'). For full details of the codes, see pp. xxxiii–xxxv below.

Readers are urged to make full use of the footnotes in any of the Recommended Texts listed just before the start of the play. They are excellent in their areas of expertise. To attempt to rival or paraphrase them would be redundant. Thus the footnotes in these scripts will hardly ever deal with word meanings and derivations; social or political history; literary derivations and comparisons; or lengthy quotations from scholars or commentators. Such information is readily available in the *Oxford English Dictionary* and from the recommended modern texts.

Generally, the footnotes in these scripts will deal with matters theatrical and textual and will be confined to three major areas: noting where and how the modern texts alter F1's line structure; showing popular alternative word readings often selected by the modern texts (these scripts will keep the F1 reading unless otherwise noted); and showing the rare occasions where and how these scripts deviate from their source texts. When the modern texts offer alternative words and/or phrases to F2-4/Qq, the original spelling and punctuation will be used. Where appropriate, the footnotes will briefly refer to the excellent research of the scholars of the last three centuries, and to possible theatrical reasons for maintaining F1's structural 'irregularities'.

The Symbol °

This will be used to show where modern texts have altered F1's line structure, and will allow the reader to explore both the F1 setting and the modern alternative while examining the speech where it is set, in its proper context and rightful position within the play. For example, though F1 is usually the source text for *Henry the Fifth* and sets the dialogue for Pistoll in prose, most modern texts use the memorial Q version and change his lines to (at times extraordinarily peculiar) verse. These texts will set the speech as shown in F1, but add the ° to show the modern texts alterations, thus:

> Pistoll   Fortune is Bardolphs foe, and frownes on him:°
> for he hath stolne a Pax, and hanged must a be:° a damned
> death:° let Gallowes gape for Dogge, let Man goe free,°
> and let not Hempe his Wind-pipe suffocate:° but Exeter
> hath given the doome of death,° for Pax of little price.°
>
> Therefore goe speake,° the Duke will heare thy voyce;°
> and let not Bardolphs vitall thred bee cut° with edge of
> Penny-Cord, and vile reproach.°
>   Speake Captaine for
> his Life, and I will thee require.°
>   (*Henry V*, These Scripts, 2.1.450–459)

Read the speech utilising the ° to mark the end of a line, and the reader is exploring what the modern texts suggest should be the structure. Read the lines ignoring the ° and the reader is exploring what the F1 text really is. Thus both F1 and modern/Q versions can be read within the body of the text.

The Vertical Line To The Left Of The Text

This will be used to mark a passage where modern editors have altered F1's verse to prose or vice versa. Here is a passage in a predominantly prose scene from *Henry V*. Modern texts and F1 agree that Williams and Fluellen should be set in prose. However, the F1 setting for Henry could be in verse, though most modern texts set it in prose too. The thin vertical line to the left of the text is a quick reminder to the reader of disagreement between Ff and modern texts (the F1 setting will always be shown, and the disputed section will be footnoted accordingly).

King Henry	Twas I indeed thou promised'st to strike,	
	And thou hast given me most bitter termes.	
Fluellen	And please your Majestie, let his Neck answere	
	for it, if there is any Marshall Law in the World.	
King Henry	How canst thou make me satisfaction?	
Williams	All offences, my Lord, come from the heart: ne-	
	ver came any from mine, that might offend your Ma-	
	jestie.	(*Henry V,* These Scripts, 4.1.240–247)

THE SYMBOL } SET TO THE RIGHT OF TEXT, CONNECTING TWO SPEECHES

This will be used to remind readers of the presence of what most modern texts consider to be split or shared lines, and that therefore the second speech could springboard quickly off the first, thus increasing the speed of the dialogue and debate; for example:

Angelo	Did I not tell thee yea? hadst thou not order?
	Why do'st thou aske againe?
Provost	Lest I might be too rash:
	Under your good correction, I have seene
	When after execution . . .

Since there is no definitive way of determining whether Shakespeare wished the two short lines to be used as a shared or split line, or used as two separate short lines, the reader would do well to explore the moment twice. The first time the second speech could be 'springboarded' off the first as if it were a definite shared line; the second time round a tiny break could be inserted before speaking the second speech, as if a hesitation were deliberately intended. This way both possibilities of the text can be examined.

THE SYMBOL → TO THE RIGHT OF THE TEXT, JOINING TWO SHORT LINES SPOKEN BY A SINGLE CHARACTER

This indicates that though Ff has set two short lines for a single character, perhaps hinting at a minute break between the two thoughts, most modern texts have set the two short lines as one longer one. Thus the first two lines of Juliet's

How cam'st thou hither. →

> Tell me, and wherefore?
> The Orchard walls are high, and hard to climbe

can be explored as one complete line (the interpretation of most modern texts), or, as F1 suggests, as two separate thoughts with a tiny hesitation between them. In most cases these lines will be footnoted, and possible reasons for the F1 interpretation explored.

THE OCCASIONAL USE OF THE †

This marks where F1 has been forced, in a crowded line, to set the end of the line immediately above or below the first line, flush to the right hand column. These texts will set the original as one complete line—the only instance where these scripts do not faithfully reproduce F1's line structure.

THE OCCASIONAL USE OF THE † TOGETHER WITH A FOOTNOTE (ALSO SEE P. XXXVII)

This marks where a presumed F1 compositorial mistake has led to a meaningless word being set (for example 'speeh' instead of 'speech') and, since there is a 'correct' form of the word offered by either F2–4 or Qq, the correct form of the word rather than the F1 error has been set. The footnote directs the reader to the original F1 setting reproduced at the bottom of the page.

PATTERNED BRACKETS { } SURROUNDING A PREFIX OR PART OF A STAGE DIRECTION

These will be used on the infrequent occasions where a minor alteration or addition has been made to the original F1 setting.

THE VARIED USE OF THE * AND ∞

This will change from text to text. Sometimes (as in *Hamlet*) an * will be used to show where, because of the 1606 Acte To Restraine The Abuses of Players, F1 had to alter Qq's 'God' to 'Heaven'. In other plays it may be used to show the substitution of the archaic 'a' for 'he' while in others the * and /or the ∞ may be used to denote a line from Qq or F2–4 which F1 omits.

THE SYMBOL •

This is a reminder that a character with several prefixes has returned to one previously used in the play.

THE VISUAL SYMBOLS HIGHLIGHTING KEY ITEMS WITHIN THE FIRST FOLIO

THE DROPPING OF THE TEXT A SINGLE LINE

This indicates where one sentence ends, and a new one begins (see pp. xvii– xviii).

THE BOLDING OF PUNCTUATION

This indicates the presence of the major punctuation (see pp. xviii–xxi).

UNBRACKETED STAGE DIRECTIONS

These are the ones presumed to come from the manuscript copy closest to Shakespeare's own hand (F1 sets them centred, on a separate line). They usually have a direct effect on the scene, altering what has been taking place immediately prior to its setting (see p. ix).

BRACKETED STAGE DIRECTIONS

These are the ones presumed to have been added by the Playhouse. (F1 sets them alongside the dialogue, flush to the right of the column.) They usually support, rather than alter, the onstage action (see p. ix).

(The visual difference in the two sets of directions can quickly point the reader to an unexpected aspect of an entry or exit. Occasionally an entry is set alongside the text, rather than on a separate line. This might suggest the character enters not wishing to draw attention to itself, for example, towards the end of *Macbeth,* the servant entering with the dreadful news of the moving Byrnane Wood. Again, F1 occasionally sets an exit on a separate line, perhaps stopping the onstage action altogether, as with the triumphal exit to a 'Gossips feast' at the end of *The Comedy of Errors* made by most of the reunited and/or business pacified characters, leaving the servant Dromio twins onstage to finish off the play. A footnote will be added when these unusual variations in F1's directions occur.)

As with all current texts, the final period of any bracketed or unbracketed stage direction will not be set.

ACT, SCENE, AND LINE NUMBERING SPECIFIC TO THIS TEXT

Each of these scripts will show the act and scene division from F1. They will also indicate modern act and scene division, which often differs from Ff/Qq. Modern texts suggest that in many plays full scene division was not attempted until the eighteenth century, and act division in the early texts was sometimes haphazard at best. Thus many modern texts place the act division at a point other than that set in Ff/Qq, and nearly always break Ff/Qq text up into extra scenes. When modern texts add an act or scene division which is not shared by F1, the addition will be shown in brackets within the body of each individual play as it occurs. When Ff set a new Act or scene, for clarity these texts will start a fresh page, even though this is not Ff/Qq practice

ON THE LEFT HAND SIDE OF EACH PAGE

Down the left of each page, line numbers are shown in increments of five. These refer to the lines in this text only. Where F1 prints a line containing two sentences, since these scripts set two separate lines, each line will be numbered independently.

On The Top Right Of Each Page

These numbers represent the first and last lines set on the page, and so summarise the information set down the left hand side of the text.

At The Bottom Right Of Each Page: using these scripts with other texts

At times a reader may want to compare these texts with either the original First Folio, or a reputable modern text, or both. Specially devised line numbers will make this a fairly easy proposition. These new reference numbers will be found at the bottom right of the page, just above the footnote section.

The information before the colon allows the reader to compare these texts against any photographic reproduction of the First Folio. The information after the colon allows the reader to compare these texts with a modern text, specifically the excellent *Riverside Shakespeare*.[7]

Before the colon: any photostat of the First Folio

A capital letter plus a set of numbers will be shown followed by a lowercase letter. The numbers refer the reader to a particular page within the First Folio; the capital letter before the numbers specifies whether the reader should be looking at the right hand column (R) or left hand column (L) on that particular page; the lower case letter after the numbers indicates which compositor (mainly 'a' through 'e') set that particular column. An occasional asterisk alongside the reference tells the reader that though this is the page number as set in F1, it is in fact numbered out of sequence, and care is needed to ensure, say in *Cymbeline,* the appropriate one of two 'p. 389s' is being consulted.

Since the First Folio was printed in three separate sections (the first containing the Comedies, the second the Histories, and the third the Tragedies),[8] the pages and section in which each of these scripts is to be found will be mentioned in the introduction accompanying each play. The page number refers to that printed at the top of the reproduced Folio page, and not to the number that appears at the bottom of the page of the book which contains the reproduction.

Thus, from this series of texts, page one of *Measure for Measure* shows the ref-

---

[7]   Gwynne Blakemore Evans, Harry Levin, Anne Barton, Herschel Baker, Frank Kermode, Hallet D. Smith, and Marie Edel, eds., *The Riverside Shakespeare* (Copyright © 1974 by Houghton Mifflin Company). This work is chosen for its exemplary scholarship, editing principles, and footnotes.

[8]   The plays known as Romances were not printed as a separate section: *Cymbeline* was set with the Tragedies, *The Winter's Tale* and *The Tempest* were set within the Comedies, and though *Pericles* had been set in Q it did not appear in the compendium until F3. *Troilus and Cressida* was not assigned to any section, but was inserted between the Histories and the Tragedies with only 2 of its 28 pages numbered.

erence 'L61–c'. This tells the reader that the text was set by compositor 'c' and can be checked against the left hand column of p. 61 of the First Folio (*Measure For Measure* being set in the Comedy Section of F1).

Occasionally the first part of the reference seen at the bottom of the page will also be seen within the text, somewhere on the right hand side of the page. This shows the reader exactly where this column has ended and the new one begins.

(As any photostat of the First Folio clearly shows, there are often sixty-five lines or more per column, sometimes crowded very close together. The late Professor Charlton Hinman employed a brilliantly simple line-numbering system (known as TLN, short for Through Line Numbering System) whereby readers could quickly be directed to any particular line within any column on any page.

The current holders of the rights to the TLN withheld permission for the system to be used in conjunction with this series of Folio Texts.)

After the colon: *The Riverside Shakespeare*

Numbers will be printed indicating the act, scene, and line numbers in *The Riverside Shakespeare,* which contain the information set on the particular page of this script. Again, using the first page of *Measure For Measure*, the reference 1.1.1–21 on page one of these scripts directs the reader to Act One Scene 1 of *The Riverside Shakespeare*; line one in *The Riverside Shakespeare* matches the first line in this text, while the last line of dialogue on page one of this text is to be found in line twenty-one of the *Riverside* version of the play.

COMMON TYPESETTING PECULIARITIES
OF THE FOLIO AND QUARTO TEXTS
(And How These Texts Present Them)

There are a few (to modern eyes) unusual contemporary Elizabethan and early Jacobean printing practices which will be retained in these scripts.

THE ABBREVIATIONS, 'S.', 'L.', 'D.', 'M.'

Ff and Qq use standard printing abbreviations when there is not enough space on a single line to fit in all the words. The most recognisable to modern eyes includes 'S.' for Saint; 'L.' for Lord; 'M.' for Mister (though this can also be short for 'Master', 'Monsieur', and on occasions even 'Mistress'); and 'D.' for Duke. These scripts will set F1 and footnote accordingly.

'Ÿ', 'W', AND ACCENTED FINAL VOWELS

Ff/Qq's two most commonly used abbreviations are not current today, viz.:

ÿ, which is usually shorthand for either 'you'; 'thee'; 'thou'; 'thy'; 'thine'; or 'yours'

w, usually with a ¨ above, shorthand for either 'which'; 'what'; 'when'; or 'where'.

Also, in other cases of line overcrowding, the last letter of a relatively unimportant word is omitted, and an accent placed over the preceding vowel as a marker, e.g. 'thä' for 'than'. For all such abbreviations these scripts will set F1 and footnote accordingly.

THE SPECIAL CASE OF THE QUESTION AND EXCLAMATION MARKS ('?' AND '!')

Usage

Elizabethan use of these marks differs somewhat from modern practice. Ff/Qq rarely set an exclamation mark: instead the question mark was used either both as a question mark and as an exclamation point. Thus occasionally the question mark suggests some minor emphasis in the reading.

Sentence Count

When either mark occurs in the middle of a speech, it can be followed by a capitalised or a lowercase word. When the word is lowercase (not capitalised) the sentence continues on without a break. The opposite is not always true: just because the following word is capitalised does not automatically signify the start of a new sentence, though more often than not it does.

Elizabethan rhetorical writing style allowed for words to be capitalised within a sentence, a practice continued by the F1 compositors. Several times in *The Winters Tale,* highly emotional speeches are set full of question marks followed by capitalised words. Each speech could be either one long sentence of ongoing passionate rush, or up to seven shorter sentences attempting to establish self-control.

The final choice belongs to the individual reader, and in cases where such alternatives arise, the passages will be boxed, footnoted, and the various possibilities discussed.

THE ENDING OF SPEECHES WITH NO PUNCTUATION, OR PUNCTUATION OTHER THAN A PERIOD

Quite often F1–2 will not show punctuation at the end of a speech, or sometimes set a colon (:) or a comma (,) instead. Some commentators suggest the setting of anything other than a period was due to compositor carelessness, and that omission occurred either for the same reason, or because the text was so full it came flush to the right hand side of the column and there was no room left for the final punctuation to be set. Thus modern texts nearly always end a speech with the standard period (.), question mark (?), or exclamation mark (!), no matter what F1–2 have set.

However, omission doesn't always occur when a line is full, and F2, though making over sixteen hundred unauthorised typographical corrections of F1 (more than eight hundred of which are accepted by most modern texts), rarely replaces an offending comma or colon with a period, or adds missing periods—F3 is the first to make such alterations on a large scale basis. A few commentators, while acknowledging some of the omissions/mistakes are likely to be due to compositor or scribal error, suggest that ending the speech with anything other than a period (or not ending the speech at all) might indicate that the character with the speech immediately following is in fact interrupting this first speaker.

These texts will set F1, footnote accordingly, and sometimes discuss the possible effect of the missing or 'incorrect' punctuation.

THE SUBSTITUTIONS OF 'i/I' FOR 'j/J' AND 'u' FOR 'v'

In both Ff/Qq words now spelled as 'Jove' or 'Joan' are often set as 'Iove' or 'Ioan'. To avoid confusion, these texts will set the modern version of the word. Similarly, words with 'v' in the middle are often set by Ff/Qq with a 'u'; thus the modern word 'avoid' becomes 'auoid'. Again, these texts will set the modern version of the word, without footnote acknowledgement.

ALTERNATIVE SETTINGS OF A WORD WHERE DIFFERENT SPELLINGS MAINTAIN THE SAME MEANING

Ff/Qq occasionally set, what appears to modern eyes, an archaic spelling of a word for which there is a more common modern alternative, for example 'murther' for murder, 'burthen' for burden, 'moe' for more, 'vilde' for vile. Some modern texts set the Ff/Qq spelling, some modernise. These texts will set the F1 spelling throughout.

ALTERNATIVE SETTINGS OF A WORD WHERE DIFFERENT SPELLINGS SUGGEST DIFFERENT MEANINGS

Far more complicated is the situation where, while an Elizabethan could substitute one word formation for another and still imply the same thing, to modern eyes the substituted word has a entirely different meaning to the one it has replaced. The following is by no means an exclusive list of the more common dual-spelling, dual-meaning words:

anticke–antique	mad–made	sprite–spirit
born–borne	metal–mettle	sun–sonne
hart–heart	mote–moth	travel–travaill
human–humane	pour–(powre)–power	through–thorough
lest–least	reverent–reverend	troth–truth
lose–loose	right–rite	whether–whither

Some of these doubles offer a metrical problem too; for example 'sprite', a one syllable word, versus 'spirit'. A potential problem occurs in *A Midsummer Nights Dream*, where provided the modern texts set Q1's 'thorough', the scansion pattern of elegant magic can be established, whereas F1's more plebeian 'through' sets up a much more awkward and clumsy moment.

These texts will set the F1 reading, and footnote where the modern texts' substitution of a different word formation has the potential to alter the meaning (and sometimes scansion) of the line.

'THEN' AND 'THAN'

These two words, though their neutral vowels sound different to modern ears, were almost identical to Elizabethan speakers and readers, despite their different meanings. Ff and Qq make little distinction between them, setting them interchangeably. In these scripts the original printings will be used, and the modern reader should soon get used to substituting one for the other as necessary.

'I', AND 'AY'

Ff/Qq often print the personal pronoun 'I' and the word of agreement 'aye' simply as 'I'. Again, the modern reader should quickly get used to this and make the substitution whenever necessary. The reader should also be aware that very occasionally either word could be used and the phrase make perfect sense, even though different meanings would be implied.

'MY SELFE/HIM SELFE/HER SELFE' VERSUS 'MYSELF/HIMSELF/HERSELF'

Generally Ff/Qq separate the two parts of the word, 'my selfe' while most modern texts set the single word 'myself'. The difference is vital, based on Elizabethan philosophy. Elizabethans regarded themselves as composed of two parts, the corporeal 'I', and the more spiritual part, the 'selfe'. Thus when an Elizabethan character refers to 'my selfe', he or she is often referring to what is to all intents and purposes a separate being, even if that being is a particular part of him- or herself. Thus soliloquies can be thought of as a debate between the 'I' and 'my selfe', and in such speeches, even though there may be only one character onstage, it's as if there were two distinct entities present.

These texts will show F1 as set.

FOOTNOTE CODE
(shown in two forms, the first alphabetical,
the second grouping the codes by topic)

To help the reader focus on a particular topic or research aspect, a special code has been developed for these texts. Each footnote within the footnote section at the bottom of each page of text has a single letter or series of letters placed in front of it guiding readers to one specific topic; thus 'SPD' will direct readers to footnotes just dealing with songs, poems, and doggerel.

ALPHABETICAL FOOTNOTE CODING

A	asides
AB	abbreviation
ADD	a passage modern texts have added to their texts from F2–4/Qq
ALT	a passage (including act and scene division) that has been altered by modern texts without any Ff/Qq authority
COMP	a setting probably influenced by compositor interference
F	concerning disputed facts within the play
FL	foreign language
L	letter or letters
LS	alterations in line structure
M	Shakespeare's use of the scansion of magic (trochaic and seven syllables)
N	a name modern texts have changed or corrected for easier recognition
O	F1 words or phrases substituted for a Qq oath or blasphemy
OM	passage, line, or word modern texts omit or suggest omitting
P	change in prefix assigned to a character
PCT	alterations to F1's punctuation by modern and/or contemporary texts
Q	material rejected or markedly altered by Qq not usually set by modern texts
QO	oaths or blasphemies set in Qq not usually set by modern texts
SD	stage directions added or altered by modern texts
SP	a solo split line for a single character (see pp. xv–xvi above)

SPD	matters concerning songs, poems, or doggerel
?ST	where, because of question marks within the passage, the final choice as to the number of sentences is left to the reader's discretion
STRUCT	a deliberate change from the F1 setting by these texts
UE	an unusual entrance (set to the side of the text) or exit (set on a separate line)
VP	F1's verse altered to prose or vice versa, or lines indistinguishable as either
W	F1's word or phrase altered by modern texts
WHO	(in a convoluted passage) who is speaking to whom
WS	F1 line structure altered because of casting off problems (see pp. x–xi above)

FOOTNOTE CODING BY TOPIC

STAGE DIRECTIONS, ETC.

A	asides
P	change in prefix assigned to a character
SD	stage directions added or altered by modern texts
UE	an unusual entrance (set to the side of the text) or exit (set on a separate line)
WHO	(in a convoluted passage) who is speaking to whom

LINE STRUCTURE AND PUNCTUATION, ETC.

L	letter or letters
LS	alterations in line structure
M	Shakespeare's use of the scansion of magic (trochaic and seven syllables)
PCT	alterations to F1's punctuation by modern and/or contemporary texts
SPD	matters concerning songs, poems, or doggerel
?ST	where, because of question marks within the passage, the final choice as to the number of sentences is left to the reader's discretion
SP	a solo split line for a single character (see pp. xv–xvi above)
VP	F1's verse altered to prose or vice versa, or lines indistinguishable as either

WS   F1 line structure altered because of casting off problems (see pp. x–xi above)

CHANGES TO WORDS AND PHRASES

AB   abbreviation

F   concerning disputed facts within the play

FL   foreign language

N   a name modern texts have changed or corrected for easier recognition

O   F1 words or phrases substituted for a Qq oath or blasphemy

QO   oaths or blasphemies set in Qq not usually set by modern texts

W   F1's word or phrase altered by modern texts

CHANGES ON A LARGER SCALE AND OTHER UNAUTHORISED CHANGES

ADD   a passage modern texts have added to their texts from F2–4/Qq

ALT   a passage (including act and scene division) that has been altered by modern texts without any Ff/Qq authority

COMP   a setting probably influenced by compositor interference

OM   passage, line, or word modern texts omit or suggest omitting

Q   material rejected or markedly altered by Qq not usually set by modern texts

STRUCT   a deliberate change from the F1 setting by these texts

ONE MODERN CHANGE FREQUENTLY NOTED IN THESE TEXTS

'MINUTE' CHANGES TO THE SYLLABLE LENGTH OF FF LINES

As noted above on pages xi–xii, modern texts frequently correct what commentators consider to be large scale metric deficiencies, often to the detriment of character and scene. There are many smaller changes made too, especially when lines are either longer or shorter than the norm of pentameter by 'only' one or two syllables. These changes are equally troublesome, for there is a highly practical theatrical rule of thumb guideline to such irregularities, viz.:

    if lines are slightly **longer** than pentameter, then the characters so involved have too much information coursing through them to be contained within the 'norms' of proper verse, occasionally even to the point of losing self-control

    if lines are slightly **shorter** than ten syllables, then either the information therein contained or the surrounding action is creating a momentary (almost need to breath) hesitation, sometimes suggesting a struggle to maintain self-control

These texts will note all such alterations, usually offering the different syllable counts per line as set both by F1 and by the altered modern texts, often with a brief suggestion as to how the original structural 'irregularity' might reflect onstage action.

FINALLY, A BRIEF WORD ABOUT THE COMPOSITORS [9]

Concentrated research into the number of the compositors and their habits began in the 1950s and, for a while, it was thought five men set the First Folio, each assigned a letter, 'A' through 'E'.

'E' was known to be a seventeen-year-old apprentice whose occasional mishaps both in copying text and securing the type to the frame have led to more than a few dreadful lapses, notably in *Romeo and Juliet*, low in the left column on p. 76 of the Tragedies, where in sixteen F1 lines he commits seven purely typographical mistakes. Compositor 'B' set approximately half of F1, and has been accused of being cavalier both with copying text and not setting line ending punctuation when the line is flush to the column edge. He has also been accused of setting most of the so called 'solo' split lines, though a comparison of other compositors' habits suggests they did so too, especially the conglomerate once considered to be the work of a single compositor known as 'A'. It is now acknowledged that the work set by 'A' is probably the work of at least two and more likely five different men, bringing the total number of compositors having worked on F1 to nine ('A' times five, and 'B' through 'E').

It's important to recognise that the work of these men was sometimes flawed. Thus the footnotes in these texts will point the reader to as many examples as possible which current scholarship and research suggest are in error. These errors fall into two basic categories. The first is indisputable, that of pure typographical mistakes ('wh?ch' for 'which'): the second, frequently open to challenge, is failure to copy exactly the text (Qq or manuscript) which F1 has used as its source material.

As for the first, these texts place the symbol † before a footnote marker within the text (not in the footnote section), a combination used only to point to a purely typographical mistake. Thus in the error-riddled section of *Romeo and Juliet* quoted above, p. 109 of this script shows fourteen footnote markers, seven of them coupled with the symbol †. Singling out these typographical-only markers alerts the reader to compositor error, and that (usually) the 'correct' word or phrase has been set within the text. Thus the reader doesn't have to bother with the footnote below unless they have a morbid curiosity to find out what the error actually is. Also, by definition, the more † appearing in a passage, the worse set that passage is.

As to the second series of (sometimes challengeable) errors labelled poor copy work, the footnotes will alert the reader to the alternative Qq word or phrase usage preferred by most modern texts, often discussing the alternatives in detail, especially when there seems to be validity to the F1 setting.

---

[9] Readers are directed to the ground breaking work of Alice Walker, and also to the ongoing researches of Paul Werstine and Peter W. M. Blayney.

Given the fluid state of current research, more discoveries are bound to be published as to which compositor set which F1 column long after these texts go to print. Thus the current assignation of compositors at the bottom of each of these scripts' pages represents what is known at this moment, and will be open to reassessment as time goes by.

A CAVEAT: THE COMPOSITORS AND 'SINGLE SPLIT LINES' (SEE PP. XV–XVI)

Many commentators suggest single split lines are not Shakespearean dramatic necessity, but compositorial invention to get out of a typesetting dilemma. Their argument is threefold:

first, as mentioned on pp. x–xi, because of 'white space' a small amount of text would have to be artificially expanded to fill a large volume of what would otherwise be empty space: therefore, even though the column width could easily accommodate regular verse lines, the line or lines would be split in two to fill an otherwise embarrassing gap

second, even though the source documents the compositors were using to set F1 showed material as a single line of verse, occasionally there was too much text for the F1 column to contain it as that one single line: hence the line had to be split in two

third, the device was essentially used by compositor B.

There is no doubt that sometimes single split lines did occur for typesetting reasons, but it should be noted that:

single split lines are frequently set well away from white space problems

often the 'too-much-text-for-the-F1-column-width' problem is solved by setting the last one or two words of the overly lengthy line either as a new line, or as an overflow or underflow just above the end of the existing line without resorting to the single split line

all compositors seem to employ the device, especially the conglomerate known as 'A' and compositor E.

As regards the following text, while at times readers will be alerted to the fact that typographical problems could have had an influence on the F1 setting, when single split lines occur their dramatic potential will be discussed, and readers are invited to explore and accept or reject the setting accordingly.

INTRODUCTION TO THE TEXT OF
THE LAMENTABLE TRAGEDY OF TITUS ANDRONICUS [1]
pages 31 - 52 of the Tragedy Section [2]
All Act, Scene, and line numbers will refer to the
Applause text below unless otherwise stated.

Current research places the play between number four and seven in the canon. It was set at the same time as the tandem plays *Coriolanus* and *Romeo & Juliet* as well as *Julius Cæsar* and *Macbeth*.

Uncertainty as to dating and authorship abound.

There are three complications as to dating. First, a Henslowe diary entry [3] for January 24th 1594 on behalf of the Earl of Sussex' men refers to a '*Titus & Ondronicus*' accompanied by the description 'ne'. Though meaning 'new', ne doesn't necessarily imply a new play but can refer to an old one newly revised or to a new play entering the repertoire, and there is a very tangled web of this play being assigned from Strange's Men to the now bankrupt Pembroke's Men and thence to Henslowe. [4] To complicate matters further, a well known reference to the play by Ben Johnson in his 1614 Introduction to *Bartholomew Fair* suggests a composition date as early as 1589.

Because of the possibility of collaborative authorship even some linguistic tests are not completely reliable: those that are place *Titus* alongside three history plays (*Henry 6 Parts Two* and *Three* and *Richard III*) and *The Taming of the Shrew*. This, together with a large cast-size (which would indicate the play being written pre-plague), point to a composition date of 1592.

---

1   Q1 is 163 spoken lines shorter. For a detailed examination, see Wells, Stanley and Taylor, Gary (eds.). *William Shakespeare: A Textual Companion.* Oxford: Clarendon Press. 1987. pages 209 - 216. For a detailed analysis of the play's contents, see any of the Recommended Modern Texts.

2   *Mr. William Shakespeare's Comedies, Histories, & Tragedies, 1623*

3   Philip Henslowe was a theatre owner and manager, the principal rival to Shakespeare's Company, the *Chamberlain's* (later the *King's) Men*: his so-called Diary is in fact, in the words of Campbell (Campbell, Oscar James and Edward G. Quinn (eds.). *The Reader's Encyclopedia Of Shakespeare.* New York: Thomas Y. Crowell. 1966), 'a folio memorandum account book which he kept from 1592 to 1603. The accounts record both his personal and business contacts with the companies he dealt with . . . The importance of his diary and papers cannot be over-emphasized': for further details of the diary see Foakes, R.A. and Rickert (eds.). *Henslowe's Diary.* 1961

4   An earlier Henslowe entry of April 11 1592 naming '*Tittus and Vespacia*' as another 'ne' play might refer to the forerunner of *Andronicus*.

As to authorship, despite the listing in Meres [5] many scholars consider Act One to be written by someone other than Shakespeare (which some linguistic tests tend to support). Interestingly, though *A Textual Companion* seems to support the idea of collaborative authorship, unlike some of the other plays its sister volumes (*The Oxford Shakespeares* [6]) attribute *Titus* to Shakespeare alone.

There is the additional problem of the so called 'Fly-scene', seen for the first time in F1, set as the end to Act Three (this text pages 50 -3). Scholars offer two possibilities; that it was added in or before 1594 by Shakespeare, thus justifying Henslowe's 'ne', or that it was added much later and not by Shakespeare. Linguistic tests suggest it is Shakespeare's, linking the scene with other early plays, not so much the Histories but more the first Comedies *The two Gentlemen of Verona, The Taming of the Shrew, The Comedy of Errours* (sic) and *Loves Labours Lost.*

SCHOLARS' ASSESSMENT

Though the source texts are few they offer complications

- Quarto 1 (Q1) of 1594, a damaged copy of which was used for Q2, Q3 and F1: it was not until 1904 that an undamaged copy was unearthed, with implications for the last moments of the play. [7]
- Quarto 2 (Q2) of 1600, essentially based on the damaged Q1.
- Quarto 3 (Q3) of 1611, which copied not only the text of Q2 but also the page by page layout.
- First Folio (F1) of 1623, which was obviously based on a theatrically annotated version of Q3, perhaps from a prompt copy. Stage directions are added; as is the 'fly' scene together with another line; Act and Scene Divisions are provided. F1 removes the occasional oath plus an extra vulgarity from Aaron (see footnote #5, page 61). There is consensus that a prompt-book holder was not involved in the annotations, for at times speech headings are too irregular and even the amended stage directions are sometimes more literary than practical.

The New Cambridge Shakespeare Titus Andronicus (see Recommended Texts below) summarises the authority question quite neatly,

---

[5] In 1598 Francis Meres registered his *Palladis Tamia: Wit's Treasury* which, among many other items, listed some if not all the Shakespeare plays that had been written pre-1598.

[6] Wells, Stanley and Taylor, Gary (eds.). *The Oxford Shakespeare, William Shakespeare, The Complete Works, Original Spelling Edition/Modern Spelling Edition.* Oxford: The Clarendon Press. 1986

[7] See footnote #3 to page 91 and thereafter, and especially footnote #7 page 94 which deals with the invented last four lines.

Both Q and F are authoritative in their exclusive spheres. The former is a 'good' quarto,[8] usually thought to have been prepared from some form of 'foul papers'. This was probably Shakespeare's working manuscript, and while he did not correct it meticulously, and the printing was less careful than we could wish, it is as close to his intentions as we can get: thus Q must be our copy text for dialogue. . . . The Folio, however, introduces new material . . . [and] . . . must be the copy-text for 3. 2 . . . I have taken Q as copy-text for stage directions, but have added those from F wherever they give a fuller sense of what is going on in the play-house. (pages 145 - 6)

The Oxford Shakespeare Titus Andronicus (single paperback version - again, see Recommended Texts below) adds a very important reminder , viz.

The great value of the Folio text to a modern editor lies in its indications, derived from the prompt book, of how the play was performed. (page 43)

THE TEXT

The play was set by compositor E (40 columns) with minor help from B (2).

F1'S STAGE MANAGEMENT OF THE PLAY

THE OCCASIONAL PREFIX PROBLEM

• THE BROTHER WHO BECOMES THE RULER OF ROME

Four different prefixes are used for Saturnine, two (Saturninus, for the first speech only, and Saturnine) reflect his given name, and two (Emperor and King) his status. At times the struggle between the personal Saturnine and the role of Emperour/King is theatrically fascinating. His first switch to Emperour is to attack Titus' family, especially Lavinia over her preference for his brother Bassianus, ('No Titus, no . . .', page 12 line 1. 1. 312), but the 'symbol of power' prefix lasts for just one speech as, seemingly in a fit of pique, he chooses Tamora to be his wife. After her superb political advice, to mask his feelings until the time for revenge is opportune, he assumes the title King and doesn't slip back to the personal until the very last line of Act One.

At the top of the supposedly peace-making hunting scene the personal is still in place and remains so, even at the news of his brother's death, until Tamora addresses him as 'my Lord the King' as she gives him the false letter implicating Titus' sons Martius and Quintus (page 35, line 2. 1. 451), at which point he adopts the formal role of/returns to the prefix King.

---

8   The term 'good quarto' refers to a script prepared and published with the full authority of the Playhouse (or individual) owning the copyright. The term 'foul papers' refers to Shakespeare's first draft, with all the original crossings out and blots intact.

Before his next appearance late in Act Four, Titus has peppered the palace with arrow-born inflammatory papers which seem to have had their effect, for the prefix of Emperour/King has once more given way to the personal Saturnine which remains in place through the discovery of the anti-Saturnine letter borne by the unfortunate Clowne and through the first greeting of Emillius, who brings news of an invading army led by Titus' son Lucius. At this news the prefix once more reverts to King as he not too successfully tries to take charge, but as soon as he is left alone with Tamora and she plans to deal with Titus, telling him 'be blithe again', the prefix once more returns to the personal (page 74, line 4. 1. 559) where it remains through all the grotesqueries of the Act Five banquet until his death at Lucius' hands.

- TAMORA'S LOVER

The character is usually referred to as Aaron (occasionally as Aron). However, in one sequence his prefix reflects his racial background, Moore, when he realises Titus has worked out Tamora's sons' guilt in the ravishing of Lavinia (page 59, line 4. 1. 158). The change seems to mark a turning point, for thereafter the character becomes openly more hostile to and alienated from all around him (save his infant son), even though the prefix reverts to Aaron four speeches later.

- AFTER THE DEATH OF MUTIUS, WHICH OF TITUS' SONS SPEAKS WHEN ?

A lack of clarity between F1 stage directions and prefixes creates a complex but minor confusion in the first scene, pages 14 and 15 this text. Commentators suggest Titus' three remaining sons are, in order of age, Lucius, Martius and Quintus, who then could be referred to as '1. Son', '2. Son' and '3. Son'. Thus on page 15, Ff assign Lucius (#1 Son) to speak first, (though Q assigns the first speech to #3 Son, Quintus) and then Martius (the #2 Son) follows with the next two speeches, a pattern followed by at least one modern text, *The New Cambridge Shakespeare*, op. cit. Inevitably, different modern texts suggest different patterns for varying reasons, often omitting Lucius entirely. The most common patterns are either Martius speaks first, followed by Quintus (*The Oxford Shakespeare*, op. cit.) or Quintus first, followed by Martius (*The Arden Shakespeare*, see Recommended Texts below).

For further details, see footnotes #2 and #3 page 14 and #1 page 15.

- THE GOTHS OF ACT FIVE

As usual in F1, generic characters are not given individual names, and in this particular play they are not even distinguished by numbers. Most modern texts set the first Goth speech of Act Five (page 75, line 5. 1. 9) for a 1st. Goth, then name the character bringing in 'Aaron with his child in his armes' the 2nd. Goth (also page 75), and assign three remaining Goth speeches late in the scene to the 1st Goth - though it would seem the Goth announcing the arrival of Emillius (page 80) may be another character altogether.

Also, most modern texts often follow Q and assign the one remaining F1 Goth speech late in the play (page 90, line 5. 1. 451) to a Roman Lord.

TWO MINOR CLARIFICATIONS

At first entry (page 72), the Roman **Emillius** is described as Nuntius Emillius: 'Nuntius' is a title meaning messenger, and not part of his name. Also the character **Boy**, appearing for the first time in the 'Fly' scene (page 50 this text), is in fact young Lucius, Titus' grandchild.

STAGE DIRECTIONS SOMETIMES NEED CLARIFICATION

• THE QUESTION OF HEIGHT: WHO IS 'ALOFT' AND WHEN

On at least three separate occasions there is no modern text consistency in assigning the 'top' spot - as seen on pages 7 and 9 with the various factions quarreling before the election of a new emperor. [9]

Then, in the famous 'revenge' sequence (starting page 80), commentators differ as to whether Titus or 'Tamora and her two Sonnes disguised' start aloft.

Finally, various suggestions are made as to who should go aloft to finish the play once all the blood-letting is done (page 90 on). While there are no 'correct' answers, whatever is finally decided will have huge implications on the staging of key moments within three very important scenes.

• NON-EXISTENT DIRECTIONS

Sometimes necessary directions are non-existent (though obvious from the dialogue) as with the deaths of Titus at the hands (presumably) of Saturnine, and the immediate death of Saturnine (again presumably) at the hands of Lucius (both page 90). And even though the moment may be obvious, sometimes incidents need more explanation, such as those surrounding the threatened hanging of the captured Aaron. [10]

• IMPRECISE DIRECTIONS

Sometimes directions are imprecise, for example after Mutius (one of Titus' sons) disobeys his father over a point of honour, the stage direction reads 'he kils him' (top of page 12), and for those fresh to the play it is not clear for several lines that it is Titus who has killed his son. Then, once the whole family has pleaded with Titus to allow Mutius to be buried in the family tomb alongside the sons who have died honourably in war, and Titus has very grudgingly agreed, F1's two directions read 'They put him in the Tombe' and 'They all kneele and say' (page 15 this text). In view of Titus' anger and reluctance, does the 'all' include him?

Then there is the question of the final moments for the Clowne (page 71), who unwittingly brought Titus' insults to the beleaguered Saturnine who has immediately ordered the Clowne be hanged. The singular 'Exit' doesn't adequately cover the situation: is the Clowne dragged offstage, or does he simply run away?

---

9 See footnotes #4 page 7 and #2 page 8.

10 See footnote #3 for page 76.

- INCOMPLETE ENTRIES AND EXITS

In the final moments of the play Young Lucius, the Boy, is asked by his father to say farewell to his murdered Grandfather ('Come hither Boy, come, come and learne of us' - page 93, line 5. 1. 538), but there is no earlier direction for his entry, and in the earlier part of the same scene, though Emillius speaks (page 92, lines 5. 1. 515 - 18), he too is not given an entry. The worst omission is that of Alarbus, the soon-to-be-sacrificed son of Tamora, the flash point for all the action: an exit direction is provided ('Exit Sonnes with Alarbus', page 5), unusual in that it is centred, and so demands extra attention, however, no prior entry was set.

- ASIDES

Provided the action of the plot is followed, asides present little problem, even in the 'revenge' sequence where at times Tamora and her two sons form one group with their own asides, and Titus (presumably with the audience) forms another (page 85). Readers should be aware of sudden switches, as the opening/closing comments of the Boy's big speech in the (amended, see footnotes #4 page 58 and #1 page 59) sequence of Titus' gift-giving to Chiron and Demetrius.

- BEWARE THE OCCASIONAL MODERN OVER-ELABORATION

A word of caution: sometimes though explaining a need, modern additions are not always timed particularly well, as with the removal of the murdered Bassianus and Titus' two sons Martius and Quintus, falsely accused of the deed (pages 35 - 7). To cause the least distraction to the on-stage action, this should be done at the end of the sequence just before Chiron and Demetrius enter with the ravished and disfigured Lavinia (see footnote #3, page 36). Surprisingly, at least one text places it some six or seven lines earlier during the King's distress. Also some additions are downright presumptuous, such as one text suggesting that as Titus cuts into the pie, the heads of Chiron and Demetrius are revealed (see footnote #7 page 89); as directorial invention this is fine, as editorial fiat definitely not.

Also, in the proposed hanging of Aaron, who orders the ladder; Aaron in a fit of bravado as set by Qq/F, or Lucius as set by most modern texts (page 76, line 54) ?

MODERN INTERVENTIONS

Since Spevack [11] suggests there are only thirty-five prose lines in the play, variations in verse and prose are infrequent. One highlights Titus' brother, Marcus, as he sets up the Clowne as a messenger from the brothers to their enemy the Emperour Saturnine (page 68, lines 4. 1. 415 - 17). In performance this moment is often cut, in part perhaps because Marcus speaks verse everywhere else in the play: but this deals a double blow as regards the audience's understanding of

---

[11] Spevack, M. *A Complete And Systematic Concordance To The Works Of Shakespeare.* (9 vols.) Hildesheim. Georg Holms. 1968 - 1980

Marcus' political acumen. First, in his only dealings with a member of the lower-class Marcus' usual verse address automatically adjusts (down?) to that of the Clowne. Second, it is him and not Titus who has the idea of needling Saturnine this way.

- **MAJOR LINE STRUCTURE ALTERATIONS**

As in most early play, these are few and far between. *A Textual Companion* lists just fourteen Q passages involving twenty-seven lines that needed to be altered for *The Oxford Shakespeares.*

One irregularity jointly set by Qq and F1 occurs as Titus organises shooting the message-arrows into Saturnine's palace. (The 'her' in the final line of the quote refers to 'Astrea', goddess of Justice, whom according to the Latin opening the speech, has already left earth.)

Terras Astrea reliquit, be you remembred Marcus.	(14 -15)
She's gone, she's fled, sirs take you to your tooles,	(10)
You Cosens shall goe sound the Ocean:	(9 - 10)
And cast your nets, haply you may find her in the Sea,	(13)
	(page 65, lines 4. 1. 323- 26)

The deranged excitement of repeated longer lines inherent in the Qq/F1 setting is palpable, so it seems a shame that modern texts replace the outbursts with hesitations by setting either

Terras Astrea reliquit,	(7 - 8)
Be you remembred Marcus. She's gone, she's fled,	(11)
Sirs take you to your tooles. You Cosens	(8 - 9)
Shall goe sound the Ocean: and cast your nets,	(11)
Haply you may find her in the Sea,	(9)

or the even more peculiar

Terras Astrea reliquit, be you remembred Marcus.	(14 - 15)
She's gone, she's fled, sirs take you to your tooles.	(10)
You Cosens shall goe sound the Ocean:	(9 - 10)
And cast your nets,	(4)
Haply you may find her in the Sea,	(9)

- **MINOR METRIC ALTERATIONS UNDERMINING F1'S LACK OF EQUILIBRIUM**

The revamping of one tiny Qq/F theatrical irregularity blurs an interesting distinction between Chiron and Demetrius. Following Aaron's explanation that, having murdered the Nurse all he has to do is kill the midwife and the fact, he, a slave, has sired a black child on the white Empress Tamora, can never be proved. Qq/F set an onrush from Chiron (admiration perhaps) and a pause and controlled highly formal 'thank you' from Demetrius

Chiron	Aaron I see thou wilt not trust the ayre with secrets.	(13)
Demetrius	For this care of Tamora	(7)
	(page 64, lines 4. 1. 308 - 9)	

The distinction between Chiron's enthusiasm and Demetrius' reserve could not be more clearly marked. Nevertheless, most modern texts destroy the distinction by regularising both lines, creating a shared line where none was originally set.

Chiron	Aaron I see thou wilt not trust the ayre	(10)
	With secrets.	
Demetrius	For this care of Tamora	(10)

Even more common are the niggling minute word or phrase adjustments to create pentameter where non originally existed, something modern texts do so often with the early plays. [12] Thus as Tamora (unsuccessfully) tries to tempt Titus to accept her in her disguise as Revenge with a promise that she will

> Provide thee two proper Palfries, as blacke as Jet   (12)
>
> (page 82, line 5. 1. 222)

the overlong F1 line betrays her overworking the image (excitement? enjoyment of the deceit?). Qq set one word less

> Provide thee two proper palfries, * blacke as jet   (11)

but some metrically strict modern texts destroy the excitement completely by removing one word more

> Provide thee * proper palfries, * blacke as jet   (10)

In other cases words are added, with the same devastation, one at a critical moment. As Marcus is about to show the tonguelesss and handless Lavinia how she can write the names of her ravishers in the sand with a stick held between her arms, both Qq and F1 set a short line

> This sandie plot is plaine, guide if thou canst   (10)
> This after me, I have writ my name,   (9)
> Without the helpe of any hand at all.   (10)
>
> (page 56, lines 4. 1. 72 - 4)

with the minute pause inherent in the second line perhaps allowing Marcus a moment to maneuver her into place: most modern texts remove the moment by expanding 'I have' to either 'I here have' or 'see I have'.

The more significant of these changes will be footnoted throughout the main body of the text.

• (THE **F1** SETTING SUGGESTING) THE OCCASIONAL NEED FOR SELF-CONTROL

Undoubtedly some **single split lines** (two or more short verse lines, set for a <u>single</u> character, which if placed together - as poets, scholars and commentators suggest - would form a single full line of verse. These lines are rarely reproduced as set by any modern text : see the General Introduction, pages xv - xvi for further discussion) are created by inadequate column width, as with the opening political addresses from both Bassianus and Saturnine (pages 1 - 2), others by white

---

[12] See the introduction to the Folio Text *The first Part of Henry the Sixt.*

space,[13] such as (perhaps) Titus' first personal greetings to his daughter and brother once the formal public ceremonies are finished (page 7).

Yet others abound that cannot be so easily dismissed, especially in the last politically charged moments of Act One after Tamora's intercession to reign in Saturnine's anger towards Titus and his family (F1 Tragedy column L 35, pages 17 - 19). The page is not immediately open to the charge of white space, and the text of no fewer than seven of the eight examples set is short enough to be set as a single line. The first three moments, of 'forgiveness' by Saturnine, and the wary public 'thanks' from Titus acknowledging the intervention of his enemy Tamora, are all wonderfully underscored with the F1 hesitations

King	Rise Titus, rise,	(4)
	My Empresse hath prevail'd.	(6)
Titus	I thanke your Majestie,	(6)
	And her my Lord.	(4)
	These words, these lookes,	(4)
	Infuse new life in me.	(6)

(page 18, lines 1. 1. 478 - 483)

as are the remaining four - the seemingly reassuring words from Tamora to Lavinia; the public apology from one of Titus' sons; Tamora's further intercession following the King's angry response to the protest from Marcus, Titus' brother; and the 'conciliation' to Marcus from Saturnine; and finally an eighth (in the first part of the next column, F1 Tragedy section, R 35, page 19 lines 1. 519 - 20 this text) from Titus offering a peace-making celebratory hunt.

All these split lines suggest enormous care and diplomacy, but they are not found in either Qq or most modern texts. The same Ff only setting is found in the gruesome teasing of Lavinia by Chiron and Demetrius (pages 30 - 2); the discovery by Martius and Quintus of Bassianus' body in the pit (page 33); and the tragic revelation of the mangled Lavinia to Titus (pages 42 - 3).

The usual minor **punctuation** changes take place, with one removal of an ungrammatical period (marked *) reducing Titus' need to pause (for self-control?) once Lavinia manages to reveal the identity of her assailants: in response to Marcus' suggestion that they publicly go after Tamora's sons, Titus comments

But if you hunt these Beare-whelpes, then beware
The Dam will wake, and if she winde you once,
Shee's with the Lyon deepely still in league.*
And lulls him wilst she playeth on her backe,
And when she sleepes will she do what she list.

(page 57, lines 4. 1. 99 - 103)

---

13 A page containing little dialogue plus empty space around it , leading modern commentators to suggest the compositors often restructured the original line sequence to create more lines than first set so as to occupy some of the blank space which would otherwise lie empty.

Whether it's the sexual imagery or the need for self-control that creates in Titus a need to pause, the moment is highly personally charged, but not so in most modern texts which follow Q in replacing the asterisked period with a comma.

• **THE ALMOST COMPLETE ABSENCE OF QUICK DEBATE**

As to be expected in an early play there are few **shared split lines**. [14] Indeed, Spevack, op. cit., suggests there are just twenty-one, several of which are to be found in the opening election debate between the two brothers contending the Emperorship. Thus, again as in early plays, discussion is more based upon characters making speeches at each other rather than engaging in the cut and thrust of debate.

THE STAGING OF THE FLY SCENE: LARGE-SCALE OR SMALL?

As in several other plays, where F1 sets a Banket (usually a light and dainty dishes for a small number of people - often just the immediate family) some modern texts set a large-scale Banquet and add Attendants. F1's misspelled 'Bnaket' suggests a much smaller occasion, and does not add any supernumeraries, (thus there are no F1 Attendants, Musicians, Servants or Others, this text pages 50 - 3).

Reader's choice will have a great impact on how the scene is to be played. If a Banket, then the pain remains contained within the immediate family only, and Titus' irrational behaviour does not become horrifyingly public. If a Banquet, then the occasion becomes more overblown, the breakdown obvious for all to see, and the scene could possibly undercut the grand guignol of the true banquet F1/Q definitively call for in Act Five.

FACTS

In *Casting Shakespeare's Plays* [15] T.J. King suggests there are 2,579 spoken lines and that ten actors can play eleven principal and two minor roles. Four boys play three principal female roles and Young Lucius[16]. Thirteen men can play six smaller speaking roles and twenty-six mutes.

The 'CATALOGUE' lists the play as *Titus Andronicus,* while the header is *The Tragedie of Titus Andronicus.* The title above the text is *The Lamentable Tragedy of Titus Andronicus.* The pages are numbered correctly. There are three catch word variations.

F1 sets Acts but no Scene Division.

---

[14] Two or more short verse lines, set for <u>two or more</u> characters, which if placed together (as poets, scholars and commentators suggest), would form a single full line of verse. See the General Introduction, pages xii - xv for further discussion.

[15] King, T.J. *Casting Shakespeare's Plays.* Cambridge. Cambridge University Press. 1992

[16] This is counting the Nurse killed by Aaron as a principal role.

Q/Ff set 'Ascend faire Queene, Panthean Lords, . . .' as if Panthean were a geographical region. Most commentators suggest this should refer to a building, The Pantheon, and restructure the text accordingly - see footnote #4 to page 13 for further details.

Finally, how many sons did Titus lose during the last war? Only 'a Coffin' is mentioned in the entry (page 3), but in the ensuing dialogue Titus refers to

> These that I bring unto their latest home,
> With buriall among their Auncestors.
>
> (page 4, lines 1. 1. 88 - 9)

and the next relevant direction refers to 'Coffins' with Titus saying

> ' . . . rest you heere my Sonnes'
>
> (page 6, line 1. 1. 156).

Neil Freeman,
Vancouver, B.C.
Canada, 1998

RECOMMENDED MODERN TEXTS WITH EXCELLENT SCHOLARLY FOOTNOTES AND RESEARCH

The footnotes in this text are concise, and concentrate either on matters theatrical or choices in word or line structure which distinguish most modern editions and this Folio based text. Items of literary, historical, and linguistic concern have been well researched and are readily available elsewhere. One of the best **research** works in recent years is

Wells, Stanley, and Gary Taylor, eds. *William Shakespeare: A Textual Companion.* Oxford: Clarendon Press, 1987.

In terms of modern **texts,** readers are urged to consult at least one of the following:

Evans, Gwynne Blakemore, Harry Levin, Anne Barton, Herschel Baker, Frank Kermode, Hallet D. Smith, and Marie Edel, eds. *The Riverside Shakespeare.* Copyright © 1974 by Houghton Mifflin Company.

Waith, E. M. (ed.). *Titus Andronicus.* The Oxford Shakespeare. 1984

Bate, J. (ed.). *Titus Andronicus.* The Arden Shakespeare. 1995

Hughes, A. (ed.). *Titus Andronicus.* The New Cambridge Shakespeare. 1994

Dramatis Personæ

THE ROMANS

The Ruling Family

BASSIANUS,
youngest son of the deceased Emperor of Rome,
in love with Lavinia

SATURNINUS,
his older brother, soon elected Emperor

The Family Andronicus

TITUS Andronicus - A Roman General

His Remaining Sons	His Other Immediate Family
QUINTUS	LAVINIA - Titus' daughter
MARTIUS	his grandson, son of Lucius,
MUTIUS	known as BOY (& Young Lucius)
LUCIUS	MARCUS Andronicus, his brother, the People's Tribune
	Publius - son to Marcus Andronicus

Kinsmen Titus Calls Upon

SEMPRONIUS   CAIUS   VALENTINE

EMILLIUS
a CAPTAINE
a MESSENGER
a CLOWNE

THE GOTHS, ENEMIES TO ROME

TAMORA, the Queene, later Saturnine's wife, and thus Empress of Rome

Her Sons

ALARBUS   DEMETRIUS   CHIRON

AARON, a Moore, her lover

Aaron's son, by Tamora

a NURSE

Romans   Goths   Souldiers   Attendants   Tribunes

This Cast List has been specially prepared for this edition, and will not be found in the Facsimile

The Lamentable Tragedy of
Titus Andronicus

Actus Primus. Scœna Prima

FLOURISH. ENTER THE TRIBUNES AND SENATORS ALOFT [1] AND THEN
ENTER SATURNINUS AND HIS FOLLOWERS AT ONE DOORE,
AND BASSIANUS AND HIS FOLLOWERS AT THE
OTHER, WITH DRUM & COLOURS

Saturnine as [2]
Saturninus   Noble† Patricians, Patrons of my right,
                      Defend the justice of my Cause with Armes.

                      And Countrey-men, my loving Followers,
                      Pleade my Successive Title with your Swords.

5   I was the [3] first borne Sonne, that was the last
                      That wore the Imperiall Diadem of Rome:
                      Then let my Fathers Honours live in me,
                      Nor wrong mine Age with this indignitie.

Bassianus   Romaines, Friends, Followers, → [4]
10   Favourers of my Right:
                      If ever Bassianus, Cæsars Sonne,
                      Were gracious in the eyes of Royall Rome,
                      Keepe then this passage to the Capitoll:
                      And suffer not Dishonour to approach
15   Th'Imperiall Seate to Vertue: consecrate
                      To Justice, Continence, and Nobility:
                      But let Desert in pure Election shine;
                      And Romanes, fight for Freedome in your Choice.

L 31 - e : 1. 1. 1 - 17

PCT [1] to separate the ritual of the opening, F2/most modern texts add a period: F1 sets no punctuation

P [2] the opening prefix for this character is 'Saturninus': virtually everywhere else, in directions, dialogue and occasional full prefix, the name 'Saturnine' is used, hence this latter will be the name this text adopts for his prefix

W [3] Qq/most modern texts = 'am his', Ff = 'was the'

SP [4] most modern texts set Qq' single line, suggesting Ff's setting of Bassianus' full name as the prefix left insufficient room for the two short lines (5 or 6/5 or 6 syllables) to be set as one: if Ff's setting stands, it might suggest Bassianus is working hard to get the listener's attention

ENTER MARCUS ANDRONICUS ALOFT WITH THE CROWNE

[1] Princes, that strive by Factions, and by Friends,
20   Ambitiously for Rule and Empery:
Know, that the people of Rome for whom we stand
A speciall Party, have by Common voyce
In Election for the Romane Emperie,
Chosen Andronicus, Sur-named Pious,
25   For many good and great deserts to Rome.

A Nobler man, a braver Warriour,
Lives not this day within the City Walles.

He by the Senate is accited home
From weary Warres against the barbarous Gothes,
30   That with his Sonnes (a terror to our Foes)
Hath yoak'd a Nation strong, train'd up in Armes.

Ten yeares are spent, since first he undertooke
This Cause of Rome, and chasticed with Armes
Our Enemies pride.
35   Five times he hath return'd
Bleeding to Rome, bearing his Valiant Sonnes
In Coffins from the Field. [2]

And now at last, laden with Honours Spoyles,
Returnes the good Andronicus to Rome,
40   Renowned Titus, flourishing in Armes.   L31 - e

Let us intreat, by Honour of his Name,
Whom (worthily) you would have now succeede,[3]
And in the Capitoll and Senates right,
Whom you pretend to Honour and Adore,
45   That you withdraw you, and abate your Strength,
Dismisse your Followers, and as Suters should,
Pleade your Deserts in Peace and Humblenesse.

• Saturnine •   How fayre the Tribune speakes, → [4]
                To calme my thoughts.

L 31 - e / R 31 - e : 1. 1. 18 - 46

[P1] most modern texts add a prefix to indicate Marcus now speaks: Qq/Ff set no such prefix

[Q2] Q1 adds the following, rarely set by modern texts
                and at this day,
      To the Monument of that Andronicy
      Done sacrifice of expiation,
      And slaine the Noblest prisoner of the Gothes.

[W3] Qq/Ff = 'succeede', one gloss = 'succeded'

[SP4] for the opening of both this and his subsequent speech, most modern texts set Qq's single line, suggesting
Ff's setting of Saturnine's full name as the prefix left insufficient room for the two short lines (6/4, and 4/6
syllables) to be set as one: if the Ff setting stands, it would suggest, for whatever reason (anger? deceit? the
need for self-control?), Saturnine frames his reply rather carefully

50	**Bassianus**	Marcus Andronicus, so I do affie
		In thy uprightnesse and Integrity:
		And so I Love and Honor thee, and thine,
		Thy Noble Brother Titus, and his Sonnes,
55		And Her (to whom my thoughts are humbled all)
		Gracious Lavinia, Romes rich Ornament,
		That I will heere dismisse my loving Friends:
		And to my Fortunes, and the Peoples Favour,
		Commit my Cause in ballance to be weigh'd.

[Exit Souldiours]¹

	Saturnine	Friends, that have beene → ²
60		Thus forward in my Right,
		I thanke you all, and heere Dismisse you all,
		And to the Love and Favour of my Countrey,
		Commit my Selfe, my Person, and the Cause:
		Rome, be as just and gracious unto me,
65		As I am confident and kinde to thee.
		Open the Gates, and let me in.
	Bassianus	Tribunes, and me, a poore Competitor.

FLOURISH
[They go up into the Senat house]

ENTER A CAPTAINE

	Captaine	Romanes make way: the good Andronicus,
		Patron of Vertue, Romes best Champion,
70		Successefull in the Battailes that he fights,
		With Honour and with Fortune is return'd,
		From whence ³ he circumscribed with his Sword,
		And brought to yoke the Enemies of Rome.

SOUND DRUMMES AND TRUMPETS. AND THEN ENTER TWO OF TITUS SONNES; AFTER THEM, TWO MEN BEARING A COFFIN ⁴ COVERED WITH BLACKE, THEN TWO OTHER SONNES. AFTER THEM, TITUS ANDRONICUS, AND THEN TAMORA THE QUEENE OF GOTHES, & HER TWO SONNES CHIRON AND DEMETRIUS,⁵ WITH AARON THE MOORE, AND OTHERS, AS MANY AS CAN BEE: THEY SET DOWNE THE COFFIN, AND TITUS SPEAKES

R 31 - e : 1. 1. 47 - 69

SD 1 most modern texts suggest just Bassianus' own 'Souldiours' (or 'Followers' as some texts suggest from the earlier dialogue) leave, and add an extra direction for the supporters of Saturnine to do likewise in four lines time

SP 2 see footnote #4, previous page

W 3 Q/most modern texts = 'where', Ff = 'whence'

SD 4 a later Ff direction (page 6 this text) states that 'Coffins' are laid 'in the Tombe'; ensuing dialogue suggests Titus buries more than one son, so at least one modern text suggests two coffins are brought on-stage: also, most modern texts name Titus' four sons, suggesting Lucius and Mutius precede the Coffins, and Quintus and Martius follow after

SD 5 considering much of the immediate action concerns itself with the ritual sacrifice of Tamora's eldest son Alarbus, most modern texts add him to the entry

3

Titus as **•Andronicus•**	Haile Rome : → [1]	R 31 - e

75   Victorious in thy Mourning Weedes:
Loe as the Barke that hath discharg'd his fraught,
Returnes with precious lading to the Bay,
From whence at first she weigh'd[†2] her Anchorage:
Commeth Andronicus bound with Lawrell bowes,
80   To resalute this Country with his teares,
Teares of true joy for his returne to Rome,
Thou great defender of this Capitoll,
Stand gracious to the Rites that we intend.

Romaines, of five and twenty Valiant Sonnes,
85   Halfe of the number that King Priam had,
Behold the poore remaines alive and dead!

These that Survive, let Rome reward with Love:
These that I bring unto their latest home,
With buriall amongst their Auncestors.

90   Heere Gothes have given me leave to sheath my Sword:
Titus unkinde, and carelesse of thine owne,
Why suffer'st thou thy Sonnes unburied yet,
To hover on the dreadfull shore of Stix?

Make way to lay them by their Bretheren.

THEY OPEN THE TOMBE

95   There greete in silence as the dead are wont,
And sleepe in peace, slaine in your Countries warres:
O sacred receptacle of my joyes,
Sweet Cell of vertue and Noblitie,
How many Sonnes of mine hast thou[3] in store,
100   That thou wilt never render to me more?

Lucius   Give us the proudest prisoner of the Gothes,
That we may hew his limbes, and on a pile
Ad manus fratrum, sacrifice his flesh:
Before this earthly[4] prison of their bones,
105   That so the shadowes be not unappeas'd,
Nor we disturb'd with prodigies on earth.

SP [1] most modern texts follow Q and set these two short lines (2/8 or 9 syllables) suggesting there was not enough column width for F1 to follow suite: if F1's setting were to stand, it would allow Titus an understandable hesitation in coming to terms with the diametrically opposed image of 'victorious' and 'Mourning Weedes' (especially given his own loss)

W [2] F2/most modern texts = 'weigh'd', F1 = 'wegih'd'

W [3] Q/most modern texts = 'hast thou of mine', Ff = 'of mine hast thou'

W [4] Q/most modern texts = 'earthy', Ff = 'earthly'

•Titus•		I give him you, the Noblest that Survives,
		The eldest Son of this distressed Queene.
Tamora [1]		Stay Romaine Bretheren, gracious Conqueror,
110		Victorious Titus, rue the teares I shed,
		A Mothers teares in passion for her sonne :
		And if thy Sonnes [2] were ever deere to thee,
		Oh thinke my sonnes to be as deere to mee.
		Sufficeth not, that we are brought to Rome
115		To beautifie thy Triumphs, and returne
		Captive to thee, and to thy Romaine yoake,
		But must my Sonnes be slaughtred in the streetes,
		For Valiant doings in their Countries cause ?
		O!
120		If to fight for King and Common-weale,
		Were piety in thine, it is in these :
		Andronicus, staine not thy Tombe with blood.
		Wilt thou draw neere the nature of the Gods ?
		Draw neere them then in being mercifull.
125		Sweet mercy is Nobilities true badge,
		Thrice Noble Titus, spare my first borne sonne.
Titus		Patient your selfe Madam, and pardon me.
		These are the [3] Brethren, whom you [4] Gothes beheld
		Alive and dead, and for their Bretheren slaine,
130		Religiously they aske a sacrifice :
		To this your sonne is markt, and die he must,
		T'appease their groaning shadowes that are gone.
Lucius		Away with him, and make a fire straight,
		And with our Swords upon a pile of wood,
135		Let's hew his limbes till they be cleane consum'd.

EXIT SONNES WITH ALARBUS [5]

Tamora	O cruell irreligious piety.

[SD 1] most modern texts suggest Tamora (sometimes accompanied by her sons) kneels to Titus

[W 2] Q/most modern texts = 'sonne', Ff = 'Sonnes'

[W 3] Qq/most modern texts = 'their', Ff = 'the'

[W 4] Q1/most modern texts = 'your', Q2 - 3/Ff = 'you'

[UE 5] set centred on a separate line as a manuscript direction (rather than to the right alongside the dialogue as a Playhouse direction), it is probable that this exit should command more attention than usual

Chiron	Was ever [1] Scythia halfe so barbarous?
Demetrius	Oppose me [2] Scythia to ambitious Rome, L 32 - e
	Alarbus goes to rest, and we†[3] survive,
140		To tremble under Titus threatning lookes,[4]
	Then Madam stand resolv'd, but hope withall,
	The selfe same Gods that arm'd the Queene of Troy
	With opportunitie of sharpe revenge
	Upon the Thracian Tyrant in his Tent,
145		May favour Tamora the Queene of Gothes,
	(When Gothes were Gothes, and Tamora was Queene)
	To quit the [5] bloody wrongs upon her foes.

ENTER THE SONNES OF ANDRONICUS AGAINE

Lucius	See Lord and Father, how we have perform'd
	Our Romaine rightes,[6] Alarbus limbs are lopt,
150		And intrals feed the sacrifising †[7] fire,
	Whose smoke like incense doth perfume the skie.
	Remaineth nought but to interre our Brethren,
	And with low'd Larums welcome them to Rome.
Titus	Let it be so, and let Andronicus
155 | | Make this his latest farewell to their soules. |

[Flourish]
THEN SOUND TRUMPETS, AND LAY THE COFFINS IN THE TOMBE

In peace and Honour rest you heere my Sonnes,
Romes readiest Champions, repose you heere in rest,
Secure from worldly chaunces and mishaps:
Heere lurks no Treason, heere no envie swels,
160 Heere grow no damned grudges,[8] heere are no stormes,
No noyse, but silence and Eternall sleepe,
In peace and Honour rest you heere my Sonnes.

ENTER LAVINIA

W [1] Q1/most modern texts = 'never', Q2 - 3/Ff = 'ever'

W [2] Qq/most modern texts = 'not', Ff = 'me'

W [3] F2/most modern texts = 'and we', F1 = 'andwe'

W [4] Qq/most modern texts = 'looke', Ff = 'lookes'

W [5] though some modern texts agree with Qq/Ff and set 'the', glosses offered include 'these' and 'her'

W [6] Qq = 'rights', F1 = 'rightes', F2/most modern texts = 'rites' - though the Qq/F1 reading has a far stronger implication

W [7] F2/most modern texts = 'sacrificing', F1 = 'saerfising'

W [8] Ff = 'grudges', Q3 = 'grudgges', Q1 - 2 = 'drugges'

Lavinia	In peace and Honour, live Lord Titus long,
	My Noble Lord and Father, live in Fame :
165	Loe at this Tombe my tributarie teares,
	I render for my Bretherens Obsequies :
	And at thy feete I kneele, with teares of joy
	Shed on the [1] earth for thy returne to Rome.

170	O blesse me heere with thy victorious hand,
	Whose Fortune [2] Romes best Citizens applau'd.

Titus	Kind Rome, → [3]
	That hast thus lovingly reserv'd
	The Cordiall of mine age to glad my hart,
	Lavinia live, out-live thy Fathers dayes :
175	And Fames eternall date for vertues praise.

Marcus	[4] Long live Lord Titus, my beloved brother,
	Gracious Triumpher in the eyes of Rome.

Titus	Thankes Gentle Tribune, →
	Noble brother Marcus.

180 **Marcus**	And welcome Nephews from succesfull wars,
	You that survive and you that sleepe in Fame :
	Faire Lords your Fortunes are all [5] alike in all,
	That in your Countries service drew your Swords.

	But safer Triumph is this Funerall Pompe,
185	That hath aspir'd to Solons Happines,
	And Triumphs over chaunce in honours bed.

	Titus Andronicus, the people of [†6] Rome,
	Whose friend in justice thou hast ever bene,
	Send thee by me their Tribune and their trust,
190	This Palliament of white and spotlesse Hue,
	And name thee in Election for the Empire,
	With these our late deceased Emperours Sonnes :
	Be *Candidatus* then and put it on,
	And helpe to set a head on headlesse Rome.

[W1] Q1/most modern texts = 'this', Q2-3/Ff = 'the'

[W2] Q/most modern texts = 'fortunes', Ff = 'Fortune'

[SP3] for the opening of both this and Titus' next speech, Ff set two short lines (2/8, and 5/6 syllables) which allow him (personal) moments of hesitation as he greets first his daughter, and then his brother: Qq/most modern texts set each pair as a single line

[SD4] most modern texts suggest Marcus (perhaps with the Tribunes and Attendants) enters (sometimes 'aloft'), often adding that he is carrying a white robe, the 'Palliament' - symbol of the office that is about to be offered to Titus

[W5] Qq/most modern texts omit this first 'all', thus setting a ten syllable line

[W6] F2/most modern texts = ', the people of', F1 sets a double comma followed by 'the peopleof'

195	**Titus**	A better head her Glorious body fits,	
		Then his that shakes for age and feeblenesse :	R 32 - e
		What should I d'on[1] this Robe and trouble you,	
		Be chosen with proclamations to day,	
		To morrow yeeld up rule, resigne my life,	
200		And set abroad new businesse for you all.	

Rome I have bene thy Souldier forty yeares,
And led my Countries strength successfully,
And buried one and twenty Valiant Sonnes,
Knighted in Field, slaine manfully in Armes,
205 In right and Service of their Noble Countrie :
Give me a staffe of Honour for mine age,
But not a Scepter to controule the world,
Upright he held it Lords, that held it last.

Marcus Titus, thou shalt obtaine and aske the Emperie.

210 **Saturnine** [2] Proud and ambitious Tribune can'st thou tell?

Titus Patience Prince Saturninus.

Saturnine Romaines do me right.

Patricians draw your Swords, and sheath [t3] them not
Till Saturninus be Romes Emperour :
215 Andronicus would thou wert [4] shipt to hell,
Rather then rob me of the peoples harts.

Lucius Proud Saturnine, interrupter of the good
That Noble minded Titus meanes to thee.

Titus Content thee Prince, I will restore to thee
220 The peoples harts, and weane them from themselves.

Bassianus [5] Andronicus, I do not flatter thee
But Honour thee, and will doe till I die :
My Faction if thou strengthen with thy Friend? [6]

I will most thankefull be, and thankes to men
225 Of Noble mindes, is Honourable Meede.

R 32 - e / L 33 - e : 1. 1. 187 - 216

[W1] Qq/most modern texts = 'don', Ff = 'd'on'

[SD 2] since Ff's next direction states 'they come down', some modern texts suggest that Saturninus and his followers appear aloft : other commentators suggest that just Saturnine and Bassianus enter above or, as mentioned earlier, Marcus and Titus are aloft and that Saturnine and Bassianus (plus their followers) enter at stage level, probably through different doors

[W 3] F2/most modern texts = 'and sheath them', F1 = 'andsheath them'

[W 4] Q/most modern texts = 'were', Ff = 'wert'

[SD 5] see footnote #2 above

[W/PCT 6] Q1/most modern texts = 'friends' (Q1 with no line ending punctuation): Q2 - 3/Ff = 'Friend', (F1 with an emphatic question mark, perhaps underlining the importance of the 'Friend', presumably Titus' brother Marcus)

Titus	People of Rome, and Noble [1] Tribunes heere,†[2]
	I aske your voyces and your Suffrages,
	Will *[3] you bestow them friendly on Andronicus?
Tribunes	To gratifie the good Andronicus,
230	And Gratulate his safe returne to Rome,
	The people will accept whom he admits.
Titus	Tribunes I thanke you, and this sure [4] I make,
	That you Create your [5] Emperours eldest sonne,
	Lord Saturnine, whose Vertues will I hope,
235	Reflect on Rome as Tytans [6] Rayes on earth,
	And ripen Justice in this Common-weale :
	Then if you will elect by my advise,
	Crowne him, and say : Long live our Emperour.
•**Marcus Andronicus**•[7]	With Voyces and applause of every sort,
240	Patricians and Plebeans we Create
	Lord Saturninus Romes Great Emperour
	And say, *Long live our Emperour Saturnine*.

A LONG FLOURISH TILL THEY [8] COME DOWNE

Saturnine	Titus Andronicus, for thy Favours done,
	To us in our Election this day,
245	I give thee thankes in part of thy Deserts,
	And will with Deeds requite thy gentlenesse :
	And for an Onset Titus to advance
	Thy Name, and Honorable Familie,
	Lavinia will I make my Empresse,
250	Romes Royall †[9] Mistris, Mistris of my hart
	And in the Sacred Pathan [10] her espouse :
	Tell me Andronicus doth this motion please thee?

L 33 - c : 1. 1. 217 - 243

[W1] Qq = 'peoples', Ff = 'Noble'

[W2] F2/most modern texts = 'Tribune s heere'

[W3] throughout the text there is evidence of what some critics term 'sophistication', i.e. Q1's 'ye' being replaced by Ff's 'you': to save a flurry of extra footnotes, from now on when such a change occurs, this script will asterisk the text accordingly without an additional footnote: the asterisk will also be set for 'thine' and 'thy', and 'mine' and 'my'

[W4] Qq/most modern texts = 'sute', Ff = 'sure'

[W5] Q/most modern texts = 'our', Ff = 'your'

[W6] Ff/Q2 - 3/most modern texts = 'Tytans': Q1 sets the interesting self-glorifying reference 'Tytus'

[P7] as Marcus formally announces the new Emperour, F1 sets the prefix 'Marcus An.', presumably his full family name: this is the only time in the play this occurs: most modern texts do not note the change

[SD8] as noted above (page 8, footnotes #2 and #5) 'They' could refer either to a combination of Saturnine, Bassianus and their followers, or to Titus and Marcus (and perhaps some Tribunes or Attendants)

[W9] F2/most modern texts = 'Romes Royall', F1 = 'Rome sRoyall'

[W10] F2/most modern texts = 'Pantheon', Qq/F1 = 'Pathan'

9

Titus	It doth my worthy Lord, and in this match,
	I hold me Highly Honoured of your Grace,
255	And heere in sight of Rome, to Saturnine,
	King and Commander of our Common-weale,
	The Wide-worlds Emperour, do I Consecrate,
	My Sword, my Chariot, and my Prisonerss,
	Presents well Worthy Romes Imperiall [1] Lord:
260	Receive them then, the Tribute that I owe,
	Mine Honours Ensignes humbled at my [2] feete.

L 33 - e

Saturnine	Thankes Noble Titus, Father of my life,
	How proud I am of thee, and of thy gifts
	Rome shall record, and when I do forget
265	The least of these unspeakable Deserts,
	Romans forget your Fealtie to me.

Titus	[3] Now Madam are your [4] prisoner to an Emperour,
	To him that for you Honour and your State,
	Will use you Nobly and your followers.

270 **Saturnine**	[5] A goodly Lady, trust me of the Hue
	That I would choose, were I to choose a new:
	Cleere up Faire Queene that cloudy countenance,
	Though chance of warre → [6]
	Hath wrought this change of cheere,
275	Thou com'st not to be made a scorne in Rome:
	Princely shall be thy usage every way.
	Rest on my word, and let not discontent
	Daunt all your hopes: Madam he comforts you,
	Can make your [7] Greater then the Queene of Gothes?
280	Lavinia you are not displeas'd with this?

Lavinia	Not I my Lord, sith true Nobilitie,
	Warrants these words in Princely curtesie.

Saturnine	Thankes sweete Lavinia, Romans let us goe:

L 33 - e / R 33 - e : 1. 1. 244 - 273

[1] Q1 - 2/most modern texts = 'imperious', Q3/Ff = 'Imperiall'

[2] Q/most modern texts = 'thy', Ff set the more self-glorifying 'my'

[3] most modern texts indicate this is said to Tamora

[4] F1 sets 'your' here and 'you' in the following line: Qq/F2/most modern texts reverse the words, setting 'you prisoner' and 'your Honour'

[5] most modern texts suggest the first two lines of the speech are spoken as an aside

[6] considering that the offer of fair treatment to the leader of an enemy might be seen as somewhat unusual, the minute hesitations offered by Ff's two short lines (4/6 syllables) are quite understandable: presumably, arguing lack of column width, most modern texts set them as one line as in Qq

[7] Qq/most modern texts = 'you', Ff = 'your'

10

Say a Bus Above
Group below w/ Lavinia until LAV. Escapes

	Ransomlesse heere we set our Prisoners free,
285	Proclaime our Honors Lords with Trumpe and Drum. [1]
Bassianus	Lord Titus by your leave, this Maid is mine.
Titus	How sir? Are you in earnest then my Lord?
Bassianus	I Noble Titus, and resolv'd withall,
290	To doe my selfe this reason, and this right.
Marcus	*Suum cuiquam,* [2] is our Romane Justice, This Prince in Justice ceazeth but his owne.
Lucius	And that he will and shall, if Lucius live.
Titus	Traytors avant, where is the Emperours Guarde?

295   [3] Treason my Lord, Lavinia is surpris'd.

Saturnine Surpris'd, by whom?

Bassianus By him that justly may
Beare his Betroth'd, from all the world away. [4]

Ex iT ?

Mutius	Brothers helpe to convey her hence away,
300	And with my Sword Ile keepe this doore safe. [5]
Titus	[6] Follow my Lord, and Ile soone bring her backe.

Mutius [7] My Lord you passe not heere.

Titus What villaine Boy,° bar'st me my way in Rome?

Mutius Helpe Lucius helpe. °

R 33 - e : 1. 1. 274 - 291

SD/OM 1 some modern texts suggest Tamora and her party are now freed from their restraints: also, both the Old-Spelling and Modern editions of *The Oxford Shakespeare*, ops. cit., suggest the two following boxed passages were originally scheduled for deletion from Q1 and that the later (modern) exit for Saturnine, Tamora, Chiron, Demetrius and Aaron (following line 304 below) should be placed here: for further details readers are directed to *Re-Editing Shakespeare*, op. cit., pages 100 - 1

FL 2 F2/most modern texts = 'cuique', Q1 - 2 = 'cuiqum', Q3/F1 = 'cuiquam'

OM 3 this and the next boxed text are the passages which *The Oxford Shakespeares* suggests cutting

SD 4 most modern texts suggest Bassianus now exits with Lavinia

SD 5 most modern texts suggest Titus' two other sons, Quintus and Martius, exit to help their sister and Bassianus

LS 6 *The Oxford Shakespeare* suggests moving this line to after the re-entry of the 'Emperour' (Saturnine) and his party, after line 312 below

SD/LS 7 instead of waiting for the Ff stage direction to occur as set (top of next page), some modern texts indicate that Titus now strikes Mutius so hard with his sword that the boy dies after his next line: also, most texts restructure the passage to two lines of regular verse (10/10 syllables) as shown: the setting of the Ff stage direction plus the three Qq/Ff lines (6/10/4) establishes a far more dramatic series of purposeful and confrontational silences, with a momentary pause either before or after Mutius' act of defiance, and again as he calls for help before his father kills him

[He kils him]

305	Lucius	My Lord you are unjust, and more then so,
		In wrongfull quarrell, you have slaine your son. [1]

Titus

Nor thou, nor he are any sonnes of mine,
My sonnes would never so dishonour me.

Traytor restore Lavinia to the Emperour.

310 Lucius

Dead if you will, but not to be his wife,
That is anothers lawfull promist Love.

**ENTER ALOFT THE EMPEROUR WITH TAMORA AND HER TWO
SONNES, AND AARON THE MOORE**

Saturnine as
•**Emperour**• [2]

No Titus, no, the Emperour needs her not,
Nor her, nor thee, nor any of thy stocke :
Ile trust by Leisure him that mocks me once. [3]

315

Thee never : nor thy Trayterous haughty sonnes,
Confederates all, thus to dishonour me.

Was none in Rome to make a stale
But Saturnine?
                    Full well Andronicus

320

Agree these Deeds, with that proud bragge of thine,
That said'st, I beg'd the Empire at thy hands.

Titus

O monstrous, what reproachfull words are these?

•Saturnine•

But goe thy wayes, goe give that changing peece,
To him that flourisht for her with his Sword :

325

A Valliant sonne in-law thou shalt enjoy :
One, fit to bandy with thy lawlesse Sonnes,
To ruffle in the Common-wealth of Rome.

R 33 - e

Titus

These words are Razors to my wounded hart.

Saturnine

And therefore lovely Tamora Queene of Gothes,

330

That like the stately Thebe [4] mong'st her Nimphs
Dost over-shine the Gallant'st Dames of Rome,[†5]

[SD] [1] though Qq/Ff set no direction, most modern texts suggest Lucius now exits, presumably to join his brothers and Lavinia

[P] [2] the first rejection of Titus by Saturnine is marked by the prefix momentarily changing from the personal 'Saturnine' to the status-emphasising 'Emperour'

[PCT] [3] F1 - 2 sets an ungrammatical period, possibly emphasising Saturnine's struggle for control: Qq/F3/most modern texts set a comma

[W] [4] F2/most modern texts = 'Phœbe', Qq/F1 = 'Thebe'

[W] [5] F2/most modern texts = 'Rome', F1 = 'R ome'

		If thou be pleas'd with this my sodaine choyse,
		Behold I choose thee Tamora for my Bride,
		And will Create thee Empresse of Rome.
335		Speake Queene of Goths dost thou applau'd my choyse?
		And heere I sweare by all the Romaine Gods,
		Sith Priest and Holy-water are so neere,
		And Tapers burne so bright, and every thing
		In readines for Hymeneus stand,
340		I will not resalute the streets of Rome,
		Or clime my Pallace, till from forth this place,
		I leade espous'd my Bride along with me,[1]
	Tamora	And heere in sight of heaven to Rome I sweare,
		If Saturnine advance the Queen of Gothes,
345		Shee will a Hand-maid be to his desires,
		A loving Nurse, a Mother to his youth.
	Saturnine	Ascend Faire Queene,[†2] → [3]
		Panthean Lords,[4] accompany
		Your Noble Emperour and his lovely Bride,
350		Sent by the heavens for Prince Saturnine,
		Whose wisedome hath her Fortune Conquered,
		There shall we Consummate our Spousall rites.

[Exeunt omnes]

	Titus	I am not bid to waite upon this Bride:
		Titus when wer't thou wont to walke alone,
355		Dishonoured thus and Challenged of wrongs?

Anger@ Son (handwritten annotation)

ENTER MARCUS AND TITUS SONNES

	Marcus	O Titus see!
		O see what thou hast done!
		In a bad quarrell, slaine a Vertuous sonne.
	Titus	No foolish Tribune, no: No sonne of mine,

[PCT] [1] F1 - 2 set a comma, perhaps suggesting in her eagerness Tamora interrupts him: Qq/F3/most modern texts set a period

[W] [2] F2/most modern texts = 'Queene', F1 = 'Qeene'

[SP] [3] Qq/most modern texts set Ff's two short lines (4/7 or 8 syllables) as one, though the pause inherent in the Ff setting creates a more formal moment between offer and command, perhaps suggesting that Tamora's response creates a need-to-breathe pause during Saturnine's reply

[PCT/W] [4] *The Arden Shakespeare Titus Andronicus*, op. cit., suggests that the Q1 compositor (and presumably of F1 too) failed to realise that 'Panthean' is a building, the 'Pantheon': thus most modern texts repunctuate as follows, 'Ascend Faire Queene, Panthean. Lords . . .'

360
>Nor thou, nor these [1] Confedrates in the deed,
>That hath dishonoured all our Family,
>Unworthy brother, and unworthy Sonnes.

Lucius
>But let us give him buriall as becomes:
>Give Mutius buriall with our Bretheren.

365 **Titus**
>Traytors away, he rest's not in this Tombe:
>This Monument five hundreth yeares hath stood,
>Which I have Sumptuously re-edified:
>Heere none but Souldiers, and Romes Servitors,
>Repose in Fame: None basely slaine in braules,

370
>Bury him where you can, he comes not heere.

Marcus
>My Lord this is impiety in you,
>My Nephew Mutius deeds do plead for him,
>He must be buried with his bretheren.

TITUS TWO SONNES SPEAKES [2]

>And shall, or him we will accompany.

375 **Titus**
>And shall!
>What villaine was it spake that word?

TITUS SONNE SPEAKES [3]

>He that would vouch'd [4] it in any place but heere.

Titus
>What would you bury him in my despight?

Marcus
>No Noble Titus, but intreat of thee,

380
>To pardon Mutius, and to bury him.

Titus
>Marcus, Even thou hast stroke upon my Crest,
>And with these Boyes mine Honour thou hast wounded,
>My foes I doe repute you every one.
>So trouble me no more, but get you gone.

PCT [1] some modern texts follow Q and add a comma, 'these, Confederates . . .', thus slowing down Titus' response

P/N [2] commentators suggest Titus' three remaining sons are, in order of age, Lucius, Martius and Quintus, who then could be referred to as '1. Son', '2. Son' and '3. Son' (as the case for #1 and #2 next page, lines 385-386, and 388): thus some critics suggest this particular stage direction might be for Martius (the number 2 Son) alone: most modern texts assign these lines to both Martius and Quintus, presumably assuming Lucius would be given his own prefix if he were to speak

P [3] most modern texts assign this to Martius, though at least one text suggests both he and Quintus speak, as before (see the preceding footnote)

W [4] Qq/F4/most modern texts = 'vouch', F1 - 3 = 'vouch'd'

385	**1. Sonne** [1]	**L·** He is not [2] himselfe, let us withdraw.
	2. Sonne	**ʌ·** Not I tell [3] Mutius bones be buried.

THE BROTHER AND THE SONNES KNEELE

	Marcus	Brother, for in that name doth nature plea'd.
	2. Sonne	Father, and in that name doth nature speake.
	Titus	Speake thou no more if all the rest will speede.
390	**Marcus**	Renowned Titus more then halfe my soule.
	Lucius	Deare Father, soule and substance of us all.
	Marcus	Suffer thy brother Marcus to interre
		His Noble Nephew heere in vertues nest,
		That died in Honour and Lavinia's cause.
395		Thou art a Romaine, be not barbarous :
		The Greekes upon advise did bury Ajax
		That slew himselfe : And [4] Laertes sonne,
		Did graciously plead for his Funerals :
		Let not young Mutius then that was thy joy,
400		Be bar'd his entrance heere.
	Titus	Rise Marcus, rise, [5]
		The dismall'st day is this that ere I saw,
		To be dishonored by my Sonnes in Rome :
		Well, bury him, and bury me the next.

L 34 - e

THEY PUT HIM IN THE TOMBE

405	**Lucius**	There lie thy bones sweet Mutius with thy friends†
		Till we with Trophees do adorne thy Tombe.

THEY ALL KNEELE AND SAY [6]

L 34 - e / R 34 - e : 1. 1. 368 - 388

P/LS [1] the logic of footnote #2, page 114, shows Ff assigning Lucius (#1 Son) to speak first, and then Martius (the #2 Son) follows with the next two speeches, a pattern followed by at least one modern text, *The New Cambridge Shakespeare*, op. cit.: Q assigns the first speech to #3 Son, Quintus: however, different modern texts suggest different patterns for varying reasons often omitting Lucius entirely - the most common patterns are either Martius first, followed by Quintus (*The Oxford Shakespeare*) or Quintus first, followed by Martius (*The Arden Shakespeare*)

W [2] Q/most modern texts set 'with', which Ff omit (creating a nine syllable line)

W [3] Q/F3/most modern texts = 'till', F1 - 2= 'tell'

W [4] Qq/most modern texts set 'wise', creating a ten syllable line: Ff omit the word

SD [5] most modern texts suggest Marcus and Titus' three sons rise

SD [6] some modern texts suggest though the rest of his family join in the ritual, Titus does not

No man shed teares for Noble Mutius,
He lives in Fame, that di'd in vertues cause.

[Exit] [1]

Marcus
410

My Lord to step out of these sudden [2] dumps,
How comes it that the subtile Queene of Gothes,
Is of a sodaine thus advanc'd in Rome?

Titus

415

I know not Marcus : but I know it is,
(Whether by devise or no) the heavens can tell,
Is she not then beholding to the man,
That brought her for this high good turne so farre?

[3] Yes, and will Nobly him remunerate.

FLOURISH .
ENTER THE EMPEROR, TAMORA, AND HER TWO SONS, WITH THE MOORE
AT ONE DOORE.   ENTER AT THE OTHER DOORE BASSIANUS AND
LAVINIA WITH OTHERS

Saturnine

So Bassianus, you have plaid your prize,
God give you joy sir of your Gallant Bride.

Bassianus
420

And you of yours my Lord : I say no more,
Nor wish no lesse, and so I take my leave.

Saturnine

Traytor, if Rome have law, or we have power,
Thou and thy Faction shall repent this Rape.

Bassianus

425

Rape call you it my Lord, to cease my owne,
My true betrothed Love, and now my wife?
But let the lawes of Rome determine all,
Meane while I am [4] possest of that is mine.

Saturnine

'Tis good sir : you are very short with us,
But if we live, weele be as sharpe with you.

Bassianus
430

435

My Lord, what I have done as best I may,
Answere I must, and shall do with my life,
Onely thus much I give your Grace to know,
By all the duties that I owe to Rome,
This Noble Gentleman Lord Titus heere,
Is in opinion and in honour wrong'd,
That in the rescue of Lavinia,

SD [1] most modern texts explain it is just Titus' sons who leave, and then have them reappear in eight lines time as
supporters of Bassianus when the two parties, of Bassianus and the Emperour Saturnine, enter

W [2] Qq = 'dririe', which most modern texts set as 'dreary': Ff = 'sudden'

P/LS [3] though Qq/Ff set this line as part of Titus' speech, some modern texts assign it to Marcus

W [4] Q1 - 2/most modern texts = 'am I', Q3/Ff = 'I am'

16

With his owne hand did slay his youngest Son,
In zeale to you, and highly mov'd to wrath.
To be controul'd in that he frankly gave :
Receive him then to favour Saturnine,
440   That hath expre'st himselfe in all his deeds,
A Father and a friend to thee, and Rome.

Titus   Prince Bassianus leave to plead my Deeds,
'Tis thou, and those, that have dishonoured me,
Rome and the righteous heavens be my judge,
445   How I have lov'd and Honour'd Saturnine. [1]

Tamora   My worthy Lord if ever Tamora,   R 34 - e
Were gracious in those Princely eyes of thine,
Then heare me speake indifferently for all :
And at my sute (sweet) pardon what is past.

450   **Saturnine**   What Madam, be dishonoured openly,
And basely put it up without revenge?

Tamora   Not so my Lord, → [2]
The Gods of Rome for-fend,
I should be Authour to dishonour you. †[3]
455   But on mine honour dare, I undertake
For good Lord Titus innocence in all :
Whose fury not dissembled speakes his griefes :
Then at my sute looke graciously on him,
Loose not so noble a friend on vaine suppose,
460   Nor with sowre lookes afflict his gentle heart.
[4] My Lord, be rul'd by me, be wonne at last,
Dissemble all your griefes and discontents,
You are but newly planted in your Throne,
Least then the people, and Patricians too,
465   ⌐Upon a just survey take Titus part, ⌐
And so supplant us [5] for ingratitude,
Which Rome reputes to be a hainous sinne. †[6]

R 34 - e / L 35 - e : 1. 1. 418 - 448

SD [1] most modern texts suggest Titus now kneels to Saturnine

SP [2] this is the first of eight pairs of Ff only short lines set in the left-hand column of page 35 of the Tragedy Section of F1, all of which Q/most modern texts set as eight single lines, though white space or inadequate column width do not appear to be serious problems on this page: here, if Ff's setting were to stand (4/6 syllables) it marks off the first moment Tamora attempts to present a public persona as a rational and diplomatic creature - and the minute hesitation as she begins is quite understandable theatrically

W [3] F1 = 'dishonouryou', F2/most modern texts = 'dishonour you'

A [4] most modern texts suggest this an aside purely for Saturnine

W [5] Q1 - 2/most modern texts = 'you', Q3/Ff set the more presumptuous and self-inclusive 'us'

W [6] F1 = 'sin.ne', F2/most modern texts = 'sinne'

Yeeld at intreats, and then let me alone:
Ile finde a day to massacre them all,
470 And race their faction, and their familie,
The cruell Father, and his trayt'rous sonnes,
To whom I sued for my deare sonnes life.
And make them know what 'tis to let a Queene. [1]
Kneele in the streetes, and beg for grace in vaine.
475 Come, come, sweet Emperour, (come Andronicus)
Take up this good old man, and cheere the heart,
That dies in tempest of thy angry frowne.

°King° [2]	[3] Rise Titus, rise, My Empresse hath prevail'd.
480 **Titus**	[4] I thanke your Majestie, And her my Lord. These words, these lookes, Infuse new life in me.

Tamora   Titus, I am incorparate in Rome,
485 A Roman now adopted happily. [5]
And must advise the Emperour for his good,
This day all quarrels die Andronicus.
And let it be mine honour good my Lord,
That I have reconcil'd your friends and you.
490 For you Prince Bassianus, I have past
My word and promise to the Emperour,
That you will be more milde and tractable.
And feare not Lords: → [6]
And you Lavinia,
495 By my advise all humbled on your knees,
You shall aske pardon of his Majestie.

[PCT] [1] F1 sets an ungrammatical period, as if Tamora is struggling to maintain self-control as she recalls the indignities done her: F2/most modern texts set a comma

[P] [2] as Saturnine begins his public deception of Titus, once more his Ff prefix shifts from the personal, this time to that status-conscious 'King': modern texts follow Qq and do not set the change

[SP] [3] Qq/most modern texts set these three pairs of Ff short lines as three single lines (3/6, 6/4, 4/6 syllables): the Ff passage shows great (diplomatic?) care as both characters try to cope with the new, dangerous, political situation

[SD] [4] most modern texts suggest Titus now rises

[PCT] [5] once again F1 sets an ungrammatical period for Tamora as she joins in the deception: F2 sets a colon, while Qq/most modern texts set a comma

[SP] [6] in view of the unspeakable horrors shortly to be inflicted upon Lavinia, the implied pause of the two short Ff only lines (4/6 syllables) has ironic and ominous overtones: Qq/most modern texts join the lines as one

Son [1]	We doe, →
	And vow to heaven, and to his Highnes,
	That what we did, was mildly, as we might,
500	Tendring our sisters honour and our owne.
Marcus	That on mine honour heere I do [2] protest.
King	Away and talke not, trouble us no more.
Tamora	Nay, nay, → [3]
	Sweet Emperour, we must all be friends,
505	The Tribune and his Nephews kneele for grace,
	I will not be denied, sweet hart looke back.
King	Marcus, →
	For thy sake and thy brothers heere,
	And at my lovely Tamora's intreats,
510	I doe remit these young mens haynous faults.
	[4] Stand up : Lavinia, though you left me like a churle,
	I found a friend, and sure as death I sware,
	I would not part a Batchellour from the Priest.
	Come, if the Emperours Court can feast two Brides,
515	You are my guest Lavinia, and your friends :
	This day shall be a Love-day Tamora. [5]
Titus	To morrow and it please your Majestie,
	To hunt the Panther and the Hart with me,
	With horne and Hound, → [6]
520	Weele give your Grace *Bon jour*.
•Saturnine•[7]	Be it so Titus, and Gramercy to.

L 35 - e (appears to right of line 512 area)

[Exeunt]

L 35 - e / R 35 - e : 1. 1. 474 - 495

P/SD 1
  Q1 sets no prefix: Q2 assigns the line to 'All', Q3/Ff simply set 'Son' without any further information: most modern texts assign the speech to the eldest son, Lucius: also, most modern texts suggest he, Lavinia, and all Titus' sons now kneel, and some suggest Marcus do so too, while others suggest he kneels as he speaks in four lines time

W 2
  Qq/most modern texts = 'doo I', Ff = 'I do'

SP 3
  in the opening of both this and the next speech, the hesitations of the Ff only short lines (2/9 or 10, and 2/8 or 9 syllables) suggest that yet again great care is being observed as the characters try to come to terms with their inner emotions and the need for public calm: Qq/most modern texts set both openings as single lines

SD/LS 4
  most modern texts indicate that all the kneelers now stand: also, Qq/Ff set a 12 or 13 syllable line, as if, just for a moment, Saturnine's emotions run away with him: most modern texts either set 'Stand up' as a separate line, reducing the line to eleven syllables, or remove the phrase from his speech, setting it as part of a stage direction

W 5
  F1 = 'Tamor a', F2/most modern texts = 'Tamora'

SP 6
  the Ff only two short lines (4/6 syllables) suggest there may be a (reluctant?) hesitation from Saturnine, forcing Titus to add the second short line: Q/most modern texts set the two short lines as one

P 7
  as the deceit ends triumphantly for the royal party, so Saturnine's prefix reverts from 'King' back to the personal

19

Actus Secunda

FLOURISH .   ENTER AARON ALONE

Aaron [1]   Now climbeth Tamora Olympus toppe,
Safe out of Fortunes shot, and sits aloft,
Secure of Thunders cracke or lightning flash,
Advanc'd about [2] pale envies threatning reach :
5   As when the golden Sunne[†3] salutes the morne,
And having gilt the Ocean with his beames,
Gallops the Zodiacke in his glistering Coach,
And over-lookes the highest piering hills :
So Tamora : [4]
10   Upon her wit doth earthly honour waite,
And vertue stoopes and trembles at her frowne.

Then Aaron arme thy hart, and fit thy thoughts,   *Erag or*
To mount aloft with thy Emperiall Mistris,   *his own*
And mount her pitch, whom thou in triumph[†5] long   *servyness*
15   Hast prisoner held, fettred in amorous chaines,
And faster bound to Aarons charming eyes,
Then is Prometheus ti'de to Caucasus.

Away with slavish weedes, and idle [6] thoughts,
I will be bright and shine in Pearle and Gold,
20   To waite upon this new made Empresse.

To waite said I?
        To wanton with this Queene,
This Goddesse, this Semerimis, this Queene,[7] *(Queen mean)*
This Syren, that will charme Romes Saturnine,
25   And see his shipwracke, and his Common weales.

Hollo,[8] what storme is this?

[P/N] [1] though the prefix usually sets 'Aron', stage directions and dialogue only refer to him five times this way, as opposed to the thirty occasions 'Aaron' is used: hence, this script will use the prefix 'Aaron' throughout

[W] [2] Qq/most modern texts = 'above', Ff = 'about'

[W] [3] F2/most modern texts = 'golden Sunne', F1 = 'goldenSunne'

[PCT] [4] F1 sets a blurred punctuation which could be a semi-colon: Qq/F2/most modern texts set a period

[W] [5] F2 = 'triumph', F1 = 'ttiumph'

[W] [6] Q1 - 2 = 'servile', Q3/Ff = 'idle'

[W] [7] Q1 - 2/most modern texts = 'Nymph', Q3/Ff = 'Queene', matching the line above

[W] [8] Qq/F1/some modern texts = 'Hollo', F2- 4 some modern texts = 'Holla', other glosses = 'Hullo' and 'Hallo'

ENTER CHIRON AND DEMETRIUS BRAVING

Demetrius	Chiron thy yeres wants wit, thy wit wants [1] edge And manners to intru'd where I am grac'd, And may for ought thou know'st affected be.
30 Chiron	Demetrius, thou doo'st over-weene in all, And so in this, to beare me downe with braves, 'Tis not the difference of a yeere or two Makes me lesse gracious, or thee more fortunate : I am as able, and as fit, as thou, To serve, and to deserve my Mistris grace, And that my sword upon thee shall approve, And plead my passions for Lavinia's love.
Aaron	Clubs, clubs, these lovers will not keep the peace.
Demetrius	Why Boy, although our mother (unadvised) Gave you a daunsing Rapier by your side, Are you so desperate growne to threat your friends?
	Goe too : have your Lath glued within your sheath, Till you know better how to handle it.
Chiron	Meane while sir, with the little skill I have, Full well shalt thou perceive how much I dare.
Demetrius	I Boy, grow ye so brave?

(In the left margin: 30, 35, 40, 45)

[They drawe]

Aaron	Why how now Lords?
	So nere the Emperours Pallace dare *you draw, And maintaine such a quarrell openly?
	Full well I wote, the ground of all this grudge.
	I would not for a million of Gold, The cause were knowne to them it most concernes.
	Nor would your noble mother for much more Be so dishonored in the Court of Rome : For shame put up.
Demetrius	Not I, till I have sheath'd My rapier in his bosome, and withall Thrust these [2] reprochfull speeches downe his throat, That he hath breath'd in my dishonour heere.

(In the left margin: 50, 55)

R 35 - e

R 35 - e / L 36 - e : 2. 1. 26 - 56

[1] Ff = 'wit wants', Qq/some modern texts = 'wits wants', one modern gloss = 'wits want'

[2] Q1 - 2/most modern texts = 'those', Q3/Ff = 'these'

21

60	Chiron	For that I am prepar'd, and full resolv'd, Foule spoken Coward, → [1] That thundrest with thy tongue, And with thy weapon nothing dar'st performe.
65	Aaron	A way [2] I say. Now by the Gods that warlike Gothes adore, This pretty [3] brabble will undoo us all: Why Lords, and thinke you not how dangerous It is to set [4] upon a Princes right?
70		What is Lavinia then become so loose, Or Bassianus so degenerate, That for her love such quarrels may be broacht, Without controulement, Justice, or revenge? Young Lords beware, and should the Empresse know, This discord [5] ground, the musicke would not please.
75	Chiron	I care not I, knew she and all the world, I love Lavinia more then all the world.
	Demetrius	Youngling, → [6] Learne thou to make some meaner choise, Lavinia is thine elder brothers hope.
80	Aaron	Why are ye mad? Or know ye not in Rome, How furious and impatient they be, And cannot brooke Competitors in love? I tell you Lords, you doe but plot your deaths,
85		By this devise.
	Chiron	Aaron, a thousand deaths ° would I propose, To atchieve her whom I do love. ° [7]

SP [1] the Ff only two short lines (4 or 5/6 syllables) and the short line opening Aaron's of following speech (4 syllables) seem to offer time for physical action separate from dialogue: Qq/most modern texts set these two lines as one

W [2] F1 - 2 = 'A way', Qq/F3/most modern texts = 'Away'

W [3] Qq/most modern texts = 'petty', Ff = 'pretty'

W [4] Qq/most modern texts = 'jet' (with the meaning of 'encroach'): Ff = 'set'

W [5] Qq/F4/most modern texts = 'discords', viz. 'discord's': F1 - 3 = 'discord'

SP [6] once more the Ff only two short lines (2/8 syllables) offer the possibility of silent physical action: Qq/most modern texts set the two lines as one

LS [7] the Qq/Ff three line passage (4/10/8 syllables) allows a pause before and after Chiron's statement, perhaps suggesting both a rather (unintentional?) comical posturing from Chiron, and deflating response from Aaron: most modern texts set two lines (10/12) as shown

Aaron		To atcheive her, how?
Demetrius		Why, mak'st thou it so strange?⁾
90		Shee is a woman, therefore may be woo'd,
		Shee is a woman, therfore may be wonne,
		Shee is Lavinia therefore must be lov'd.
		What man, more water glideth by the Mill
		Then wots the Miller of, and easie it is
95		Of a cut loafe to steale a shive we know:
		Though Bassianus be the Emperours brother,
		Better then he have worne Vulcans badge,¹
Aaron	²	I, and as good as Saturnius³ may.
Demetrius		Then why should he dispaire that knowes to court it †
100		With words, faire lookes, and liberality:
		What hast not thou full often strucke a Doe,
		And borne her cleanly by the Keepers nose?
Aaron		Why then it seemes some certaine snatch or so
		Would serve your turnes.
105	**Chiron**	I so the turne were served.⁾
Demetrius		Aaron thou hast hit it.
Aaron		Would you had hit it too,⁾
		Then should not we be tir'd with this adoo:
		Why harke yee, harke yee, and†⁴ are you such fooles,
110		To square for this?
		Would it offend you then?
		∞⁵
Chiron		Faith not me.
Demetrius		Not me, so I were one.⁾
Aaron		For shame be friends, & joyne for that†⁶ you jar:
115		'Tis pollicie, and stratageme must doe
		That you affect, and so must you resolve, L 36 - e

L 36 - e : 2. 1. 81 - 105

ᴾᶜᵀ ₁ F1 sets blurred punctuation which could be a comma, suggesting Demetrius just takes a breath (allowing Aaron his aside - see the following footnote) before continuing: Qq/F2 set a period

ᴬ ₂ most modern texts suggest this is spoken as an aside

ᵂ ₃ Qq/F2/most modern texts = 'Saturninus', F1 = 'Saturnius'

ᵂ ₄ F2/most modern texts = 'and', F1 = 'aud'

ᴬᴰᴰ ₅ most modern texts add a half line set by Qq and omitted by Ff, 'That both should speede.'

ᵂ ₆ F2/most modern texts = 'that', F1 = 'th at'

That what you cannot as you would atcheive,
   — You must perforce accomplish as you may:
Take this of me, Lucrece was not more chast
120   Then this Lavinia, Bassianus love,
A speedier course this [1] lingring languishment
Must we pursue, and I have found the path:
My Lords, a solemne hunting is in hand.

There will the lovely Roman Ladies troope:
125   The Forrest walkes are wide and spacious,
And many unfrequented plots there are,
Fitted by kinde for rape and villanie:
Single you thither then this dainty Doe,
And strike her home by force, if not by words:
130   This way or not at all, stand you in hope.

Come, come, our Empresse with her sacred wit
To villainie and vengance consecrate,
Will we acquaint with all that [2] we intend,
And she shall file our engines with advise,
135   That will not suffer you to square your selves,
But to your wishes height advance you both.

The Emperours Court is like the house of Fame,
The pallace full of tongues, of eyes, of [3] eares:
The Woods are ruthlesse, dreadfull, deafe, and dull:
140   There speake, and strike brave Boyes, & take your turnes.

There serve your lusts,[4] shadow'd from heavens eye,
And revell in Lavinia's Treasurie. [5]

Chiron   Thy counsell Lad smells of no cowardise.

Demetrius   *Sy fas* [6] *aut nefas,* till I find the streames,[7]
145   To coole this heat, a Charme to calme their [8] fits,
Per Stigia per manes Vehor. [9]

R 36 - e : 2. 1. 106 - 135

W [1] Qq/Ff = 'this', most modern texts set the gloss 'than'

W [2] Qq/some modern texts = 'withall what', Ff = 'with all that', some modern texts = 'with all what'

W [3] Q1 - 2/most modern texts = ', and', though most modern texts drop the preceding comma: Q3/Ff = ', of'

W [4] Qq/most modern texts = 'lust', Ff = 'lusts'

W [5] F1 = 'Treasur ie', F2/most modern texts = 'Treasurie'

FL [6] F1 = 'Sy', F2-4 = 'Si', most modern texts = 'Sit'

W [7] Qq/most modern texts = 'streame', F1 = 'streames'

W [8] Qq/most modern texts = 'these', Ff = 'their'

FL/W [9] noting that the quotation comes from Seneca's Phædra, most modern texts set the correct Latin, viz. 'Per Stygia, per amnes igneos amens sequar.'

[Exeunt]
**ENTER TITUS ANDRONICUS AND HIS THREE SONNES, MAKING A NOYSE
WITH HOUNDS AND HORNES, AND MARCUS**
[Most modern texts create a new scene here, Act Two Scene 2]

Titus	The hunt is up, the morne [1] is bright and gray,
	The fields are fragrant, and the Woods are greene,
	Uncouple heere, and let us make a bay,
150	And wake the Emperour, and his lovely Bride,
	And rouze the Prince, and ring a hunters peale,
	That all the Court may eccho with the noyse.

Sonnes let it be your charge, as it is ours,
To attend the Emperours person carefully:
155   I have bene troubled in my sleepe this night,
But dawning day new comfort hath inspir'd.

WINDE HORNES.
**HEERE A CRY OF HOUNDES, AND WINDE HORNES IN A PEALE, THEN
ENTER SATURNINUS, TAMORA, BASSIANUS, LAVINIA, CHIRON, DE-
METRIUS, AND THEIR ATTENDANTS**

Titus	Many good morrowes to your Majestie,
	Madam to you as many and[†2] as good.
	I promised your Grace, a Hunters peale.
160 **Saturnine**	And you have rung it lustily my Lords,
	Somewhat to earely for new married Ladies.
Bassianus	Lavinia, how say you?
	}
Lavinia	I say no:
	I have bene [3] awake two houres and more.
165 **Saturnine**	Come on then, horse and Chariots let us[†4] have,
	And to our sport: Madam, now shall ye see,
	Our Romaine hunting.
	}
Marcus	I have dogges my Lord,
	Will rouze the proudest Panther in the Chase,
170	And clime the highest Promontary[†5] top.

[W/F 1] Q3/Ff/most modern texts = 'morne': Q1 - 2 offer the intriguing possibility of a night hunt by setting 'Moone', thus adding more plausibility both for the amorous meeting of Aaron and Tamora, and the device of Martius falling into the 'panther' trap: this could also give credence to Martius' later comment of preferring to 'leave our sport to sleepe a while', line 385, page 33, and Saturnine's 'too early' remark, line 161 this page: (Titus' 'dawning-day' reference at the end of this speech could well refer to the just breaking dawn rather than dawn having already arrived)

[W 2] F2/most modern texts = 'many and', F1 = 'manyand'

[W 3] Qq/some modern texts add 'broad' (creating an eleven syllable line), which Ff omit

[W 4] F1 = 'letus', F2/most modern texts = 'let us'

[W 5] F1 = 'Pomontary', F2/most modern texts = 'Promontory'

| Titus | And I have horse will follow where the game |
| | Makes way, and runnes likes [1] Swallowes ore the plaine [2]   R 36 - e |

| Demetrius | Chiron we hunt not we, with Horse nor Hound |
| | But hope to plucke a dainty Doe to ground. |

[Exeunt]
ENTER AARON ALONE [3]
[Most modern texts create a new scene here, Act Two Scene 3]

175 **Aaron**   He that had wit, would thinke that I had none,
To bury so much Gold under a Tree,
And never after to inherit it.

Let him that thinks of me so abjectly,
Know that this Gold must coine a stratageme,
180 Which cunningly effected, will beget
A very excellent peece of villany :
And so repose sweet Gold for their unrest,
That have their Almes out of the Empresse Chest.

ENTER TAMORA TO THE MOORE [4]

Tamora   My lovely Aaron, → [5]
185 Wherefore look'st thou sad,
When every thing doth make a Gleefull boast?

The Birds chaunt melody on every bush,
The Snake lies rolled in the chearefull Sunne,
The greene leaves quiver. [6] with the cooling winde,
190 And make a cheker'd shadow on the ground :
Under their sweete shade, Aaron let us sit,
And whil'st the babling Eccho mock's the Hounds,
Replying shrilly to the well tun'd-Hornes,
As if a double hunt were heard at once,
195 Let us sit downe, and marke their yelping [7] noyse :
And after conflict, such as was suppos'd. [8]

[W][1] Ff = 'runnes likes', Qq/most modern texts = 'runnes like'

[PCT][2] probably because of lack of column width F1 sets no punctuation : if this should stand, it might suggest Titus is exiting as he speaks

[SD][3] since during his first speech Aaron describes burying gold, most modern texts indicate he is carrying it in with him

[W][4]
[SP][5] Qq/most modern texts add that Tamora is 'alone'

[6] Ff's two short lines opening Tamora's speech and Aaron's next page reply (5/5, and 2/8 syllables) allow a silent moment for them to embrace or kiss (or for Aaron to avoid embracing and/or kissing, hence the second short line) : Qq/most modern texts set each pair of lines as one single line

[PCT][6] F1 - 2 set a totally ungrammatical period, which, if it were to stand, might suggest the 'Snake' isn't the only thing that is quivering : Qq/F3/most modern texts omit the punctuation

[W][7] Qq/most modern texts = 'yellowing', Ff = 'yelping'

[PCT][8] see footnote #6 above

26

The wandring Prince and Dido once enjoy'd,
When with a happy storme they were surpris'd,
And Curtain'd with a Counsaile-keeping Cave,
200   We may each wreathed in the others armes,
(Our pastimes done) possesse a Golden slumber,
Whiles Hounds and Hornes, and sweet Melodious Birds
Be unto us, as is a Nurses Song
Of Lullabie, to bring her Babe asleepe.

205   **Aaron**   Madame, →
Though Venus governe your desires,
Saturne is Dominator over mine :
What signifies my deadly standing eye,
My silence, and my Cloudy Melancholie,
210   My fleece of Woolly haire, that now uncurles,
Even as an Adder when she doth unrowle
To do some fatall execution?

No Madam, these are no Veneriall signes,
Vengeance is in my heart, death in my hand,
215   Blood, and revenge, are Hammering in my head.

Harke Tamora, the Empresse of my Soule,
Which never hopes more heaven, then rests in thee,
This is the day of Doome for Bassianus ;
His Philomel must loose her tongue to day,
220   Thy Sonnes make Pillage of her Chastity,
And wash their hands in Bassianus blood.

Seest thou this Letter, take it up I pray thee,
And give the King this fatall plotted Scrowle,
Now question me no more, we are espied,
225   Heere comes a parcell of our hopefull Booty,
Which dreads not yet their lives destruction.

ENTER BASSIANUS AND LAVINIA

    Tamora   Ah my sweet Moore : → [1]
Sweeter to me then life.

    Aaron   No more great Empresse, Bassianus comes,
230   Be crosse with him, and Ile goe fetch thy Sonnes
To backe thy quarrell [2] what so ere they be. [3]

L 37 - e : 2. 3. 22 - 54

[SP] [1] as with the previous Ff only pair of short lines (footnote #5, page 26), this and the one following could serve to cover physical activity, the first (4/6 syllables) an embrace, the second (next page) a scrambling apart as Bassianus and Lavinia discover the amorous pair (4/5 syllables): Qq/most modern texts set each pair as one single line

[W] [2] Q1 - 2/most modern texts = 'quarrels', Q3/Ff = 'quarrell'

[SD] [3] most modern texts suggest Aaron now leaves

Bassianus	Whom [1] have we heere? →
	Romes Royall Empresse, *L37 - e*
	Unfurnisht of our [2] well beseeming troope? →
235	Or is it Dian habited like her,
	Who hath abandoned her holy Groves,
	To see the generall Hunting in this Forrest?
Tamora	Sawcie controuler of our [3] private steps:
	Had I the power, the some say Dian had,
240	Thy Temples should be planted presently. [4]
	With Hornes, as was Acteons, and the [5] Hounds
	Should drive [6] upon his new transformed limbes,
	Unmannerly Intruder as thou art.
Lavinia	Under your patience gentle Empresse,
245	'Tis thought you have a goodly gift in Horning,
	And to be doubted, that your Moore and you
	Are singled forth to try [7] experiments:
	Jove sheild your husband from his Hounds to day,
	'Tis pitty they should take him for a Stag.
250 **Bassianus**	Beleeve me Queene, your swarth [8] Cymerion,
	Doth make you Honour of his bodies Hue,
	Spotted, detested, and abhominable.
	Why are you sequestred from all your traine?
	Dismounted from your Snow-white goodly Steed,
255	And wandred hither to an obscure plot,
	Accompanied [9] with a barbarous Moore,
	If foule desire had not conducted you?
Lavinia	And being intercepted in your sport,

L 37 - e / R 37 - e : 2. 3. 55 - 80

[1] Qq/most modern texts = 'Who', Ff = 'Whom'

[2] Q1 - 2/most modern texts = 'her', Q3/Ff = 'our'

[3] Q1 - 2/most modern texts = 'my', Q3/Ff = 'our'

[4] as seen several times already, F1 - 2 set an ungrammatical period suggesting a struggle to maintain self-control: Qq/F3/most modern texts set a comma

[5] Qq/Ff/most modern texts = 'the', one modern gloss = 'thy'

[6] Qq/Ff/most modern texts = 'drive', one modern gloss suggests the highly evocative 'dine'

[7] some modern texts add Q1's 'thy' even though this creates an eleven syllable line: other texts follow Q2 - 3/Ff and omit the word

[8] Q1 - 2 = 'swartie', Q3 = 'swarty' (all setting an eleven syllable line): Ff = 'swarth': modern glosses = 'swart' and 'swarthy'

[9] Q1 - 2/most modern texts set 'but', creating an eleven syllable line: Q3/Ff omit the word

28

		Great reason that my Noble Lord, be rated
260		For Saucinesse, I pray you let us hence,
		And let her joy her Raven coloured love,
		This valley fits the purpose passing well.

Bassianus   The King my Brother shall have notice [1] of this.

Lavinia   I, for these slips have made him noted long,
265   Good King, to be so mightily abused.

Tamora   Why I have [2] patience to endure all this?

ENTER CHIRON AND DEMETRIUS

Demetrius   How now deere Soveraigne → [3]
And our gracious Mother,
Why doth your Highnes looke so pale and wan?

270 **Tamora**   Have I not reason thinke you to looke pale.

These two have tic'd me hither to this place,
A barren, detested vale you see it is.

The Trees though Sommer, yet forlorne and leane,
Ore-come [4] with Mosse, and balefull Misselto.

275   Heere never shines the Sunne, heere nothing breeds,
Unlesse the nightly Owle, or fatall Raven:
And when they shew'd me this abhorred pit,
They told me heere at dead time of the night,
A thousand Fiends, a thousand hissing Snakes,
280   Ten thousand swelling Toades, as many Urchins,
Would make such fearefull and confused cries,
As any mortall body hearing it,
Should straite fall mad, or else die suddenly.

No sooner had they told this hellish tale,
285   But strait they told me they would binde me heere,
Unto the body of a dismall yew,
And leave me to this miserable death.

And then they call'd me foule Adulteresse,
Lascivious Goth, and all the bitterest tearmes
290   That ever eare did heare to such effect.

[W][1] Qq/Ff set 'notice', creating an eleven syllable line: commentators suggest emending this to 'note'

[W][2] Qq/F1 = 'I have', F2 = 'have I': most modern texts set Qq/F1, adding a comma after 'Why'

[SP][3] the Ff only two short lines (5 or 6/syllables) allow Demetrius to see something is amiss before he continues: Qq/most modern texts set the two lines as one

[W][4] Q1/some modern texts set 'Overcome', an eleven syllable line: Q2 - 3/Ff/other modern texts = 'Ore-come'

And had you not by wondrous fortune come,
This vengeance on me had they executed:
Revenge it, as you love your Mothers life,
Or be ye not henceforth cal'd my Children.

295 **Demetrius** This is a witnesse that I am thy Sonne.

[stab him] *over & over*

Chiron And this for me, → [1]
Strook home to shew my strength

Lavinia I come Semeramis nay Barbarous Tamora. R 37 - e
evil Queen
For no name fits thy nature but thy owne.

300 **Tamora** Give me thy [2] poyniard, you shal know my boyes
Your Mothers hand shall right your Mothers wrong.

Demetrius Stay Madam heere is more belongs to her,
First thrash the Corne, then after burne the straw:
This Minion stood upon her chastity,
305 Upon her Nuptiall vow, her loyaltie.

And with that painted [3] hope, braves your Mightinesse,
And shall she carry this unto her grave?

Chiron And if she doe, → [4]
I would I were an Eunuch,
310 Drag hence her husband to some secret hole,
And make his dead Trunke-Pillow to our lust.

Tamora But when ye have the hony we [5] desire,
Let not this Waspe out-live us both to sting.

Chiron I warrant you Madam we will make that sure:
315 Come Mistris, now perforce we will enjoy,
That nice-preserved honesty of yours.

Lavinia Oh Tamora, thou bear'st a woman [6] face.

R 37 - e / L 38 - e : 2. 3. 112 - 136

SP/SD [1] the Ff only two short lines (4/6 syllables) allow a pause for Chiron to stab Bassianus before continuing:
Qq/most modern texts set the two lines as one, often suggesting they both stab Bassianus after Chiron's line
(thus denying the Qq/Ff stage direction): some texts also suggest Tamora makes a move towards Lavinia, thus
generating Lavinia's next line

W [2] Q1 - 2/most modern texts = 'the', Q3/Ff = 'thy'

W [3] Qq/Ff/most modern texts = 'painted': modern glosses = 'quaint' and 'pall'd'

SP [4] this is the first of ten Ff only paired short lines on this page, #38 of the Tragedy Section of F1, four in the left
column, six in the right: Qq/most modern texts set each pair as a single line: here, if the Ff setting stands (4/7
syllables), the pause engendered allows Chiron to make a quiet (purposeful?) move towards Lavinia

W [5] F2/most modern texts 'ye', Qq/F1 = 'we'

W [6] Q1/most modern texts = 'womans', Q2 - 3/Ff = 'woman'

30

	Tamora	I will not heare her speake, away with her.
	Lavinia	Sweet Lords intreat her heare me but a word.
320	**Demetrius**	Listen faire Madam, let it be your glory To see her teares, but be your hart to them, As unrelenting flint to drops of raine.
	Lavinia	When did the Tigers young-ones teach the dam?
325		O doe not learne her wrath, she taught it thee, The milke thou suck'st from her did turne to Marble, Even at thy Teat thou had'st thy Tyranny, Yet every Mother breeds not Sonnes alike, ¹ Do thou intreat her shew a woman ² pitty.
330	**Chiron**	What, → ³ Would'st thou have me prove my selfe a bastard?
335	**Lavinia**	'Tis true, → ⁴ The Raven doth not hatch a Larke, Yet have I heard, Oh could I finde it now, The Lion mov'd with pitty, did indure To have his Princely pawes par'd all away.
		Some say, that Ravens foster forlorne children, The whil'st their owne birds famish in their nests: Oh be to me though thy hard hart say no, Nothing so kind but something pittifull.
340	**Tamora**	I know not what it meanes, away with her.
	Lavinia	Oh let me teach thee for my Fathers sake, That gave thee life when well he might have slaine thee: Be not obdurate, open thy deafe eares.
345	**Tamora**	Had'st thou in person nere offended me. ⁵ Even for his sake am I pittilesse: Remember Boyes I powr'd forth teares in vaine, To save your brother from the sacrifice, But fierce Andronicus would not relent,

---

^{WHO} ₁ since Chiron is next to speak, some modern texts suggest Lavinia addresses this to him, though there is no reason why she shouldn't say it to both sons

^W ₂ Q1/most modern texts = 'womans', Q2 - 3/Ff = 'woman'

^{SP} ₃ this pair of Ff only short lines (1/10 syllables) allows Chiron to play with Lavinia's hopes

^{SP} ₄ this pair of Ff only short lines (2/7 or 8 syllables) might well indicate Lavinia's attempts to stay calm and dignified despite all that is taking place about her

^{PCT} ₅ once again F1 sets an ungrammatical period which, if it were to stand, would once again suggest a struggle for Tamora to maintain self-control: Qq/F2/most modern texts set a comma

2. 1. 349 - 376

		Therefore away with her, and use her as you will,
350		The worse to her, the better lov'd of me.
	Lavinia	Oh Tamora, → [1] Be call'd a gentle Queene, And with thine owne hands kill me in this place, For 'tis not life that I have beg'd so long,
355		Poore I was slaine, when Bassianus dy'd.
	Tamora	What beg'st thou then? fond woman let me go?
	Lavinia	'Tis present death I beg, and one thing more, That womanhood denies my tongue to tell : Oh keepe me from their worse then killing lust,
360		And tumble me into some loathsome pit, Where never mans eye may behold my body, Doe this, and be a charitable murderer.
	Tamora	So should I rob my sweet Sonnes of their fee, No let them satisfie [2] their lust on thee.
365	**Demetrius**	Away, → [3] For thou hast staid us heere too long.
	Lavinia	No Grace,†[4] → No womanhood? Ah beastly creature,
370		The blot and enemy to our generall name, Confusion fall ——
	Chiron	Nay then Ile stop your mouth → [5] Bring thou her husband, This is the Hole where Aaron bid us hide him. [6]
375	**Tamora**	Farewell my Sonnes, see that you make her sure, Nere let my heart know merry cheere indeed,

L 38 - e

L 38 - e / R 38 - e : 2. 3. 166 - 188

SP [1] the hesitations inherent in this pair of Ff only short lines (4/6 syllables) could serve to show how delicately and carefully Lavinia is trying to find a way to appeal to the 'queenly' and the 'gentle' nature of Tamora

W [2] Q1 = 'satisfee', Q2 - 3/Ff/most modern texts = 'satisfie': *The Arden Shakespeare*, op. cit., sets 'satisfice', explaining it is 'an authentic sixteenth-century compound from 'satisfy' and 'suffice''

SP [3] the two pairs of Ff only short lines (2/8 and 2/9 syllables) allow silent moments for the manhandling of Lavinia: Qq/most modern texts set the four lines as two

W [4] F2/most modern texts = 'Grace', F1 = 'Garace'

SP [5] the two short Ff lines (6/5 syllables) create tiny non-spoken moments both at the end of the first line for Chiron to put his hand over Lavinia's mouth, and after the second for him to begin to take her off-stage as Demetrius moves towards her late husband's body: though at least one modern text sets the Ff layout as shown: most modern texts follow Qq and set the two lines as one

SD [6] most modern texts indicate that the two men leave with Lavinia, having thrown Bassianus' body into the pit

Till all the Andronici be made away :
Now will I hence to seeke my lovely Moore,
And let my spleenefull Sonnes this Trull defloure.

Lewd~worthless
[Exit]   *Female*
ENTER AARON WITH TWO OF TITUS SONNES [1]

380   **Aaron**   Come on my Lords, the better foote before,
                        Straight will I bring you to the lothsome pit,
                        Where I espied the Panther fast asleepe.

         Quintus   My sight is very dull what ere it bodes.

         Martius   And mine I promise you, were it not for shame,
385   Well could I leave our sport to sleepe a while.

         Quintus   What are thou fallen? → [2]

                        What subtile Hole is this,
                        Whose mouth is covered with Rude growing Briers,
                        Upon whose leaves are drops of new-shed-blood,
390   As fresh as mornings [3] dew distil'd on flowers,
                        A very fatall place it seemes to me :
                        Speake Brother hast thou hurt thee with the fall?

         Martius   Oh Brother, → [4]
                        With the dismal'st object [5]
395   That ever eye with sight made heart lament.

         Aaron   Now will I fetch the King to finde them heere,
                        That he thereby may have a likely gesse,
                        How these were they that made away his Brother.

                        [Exit Aaron]

         Martius   Why dost not comfort me and helpe me out,
400   From this unhallow'd and blood-stained Hole?

         Quintus   I am surprised with an uncouth feare,
                        A chilling sweat ore-runs my trembling joynts,
                        My heart suspects more then mine eie can see.

R 38 - e : 2. 3. 189 - 213

SD [1] most modern texts give the names of 'Titus Sonnes', Quintus and Martius

SP [2] the Ff only two short lines (4 or 5/6 syllables) could allow for both Martius' fall and a moment (of shock? despair?) as Quintus realises what has happened: most modern texts follow Qq and set the two lines as one

W [3] Q1 - 2/most modern texts = 'morning', Q3/Ff = 'mornings'

SP [4] the two Ff only short lines (3/6 syllables) can create great dramatic effect, offering a hesitation before the reply (leaving the audience/Quintus to wonder whether Martius is safe), and during, as Martius copes with the horror before him: most modern texts follow Qq and set the two lines as one

W [5] Q1 - 2 sets 'hurt', which Q3/Ff omit

	Martius	To prove thou hast a true divining heart,
405		Aaron and thou looke downe into this den,
		And see a fearefull sight of blood and death.

Quintus   Aaron is gone, → [1]
And my compassionate heart
Will not permit mine eyes once to behold
410   The thing where at it trembles by surmise:
Oh tell me how [2] it is, for nere till now
Was I a child, to feare I know not what.

Martius   Lord Bassianus lies embrewed heere,[3]
All on a heape like to the [4] slaughtred Lambe,
415   In this detested, darke, blood-drinking pit.

Quintus   If it be darke, how doost thou know 'tis he?

Martius   Upon his bloody finger he doth weare
A precious Ring, that lightens all the [5] Hole:
Which like a Taper in some Monument,
420   Doth shine upon the dead mans earthly [6] cheekes,
And shewes the ragged intrailes of the [7] pit [†]:
So pale did shine the Moone on Piramus,[8]
When he by night lay bath'd in Maiden blood: [†9]
O Brother helpe me with thy fainting hand. [10]
425   If feare hath made thee faint as mee it hath,
Out of this fell devouring receptacle,
As hatefull as Ocitus [11] mistie mouth.

R 38 - e : 2. 3. 214 - 236

SP [1] this is the final pair of Ff only short lines on page #38 (4/6 syllables): given Quintus' dialogue of admitting his fear, the hesitations might suggest he is having difficulty in maintaining self-control: most modern texts follow Qq and set the two lines as one

W [2] Q1 - 2/most modern texts = 'who', Q3/Ff = 'how'

W [3] the photostat of Q1 used in *Shakespeare's Plays in Quarto*, op. cit., shows the phrase 'bereavd in blood' struck through with a hand-drawn dash and a somewhat illegible correction in manuscript hand: Q2 - 3/Ff = 'embrewed heere': most modern texts set the gloss 'berayed in blood'

W [4] Qq/most modern texts = 'a', Ff = 'the'

W [5] Q1 - 2/most modern texts = 'this', Q3/Ff = 'the'

W [6] Q1 - 2/most modern texts = 'earthy', Q3/Ff = 'earthly'

W [7] Qq/most modern texts = 'this', Ff = 'the', with F2 setting 'pit', F1 = 'p it'

W [8] Q2 - 3/Ff/most modern texts = 'Piramus. Q1 = 'Priamus'

W [9] F2/most modern texts = 'blood', F1 = 'b lood'

PCT [10] F1 sets an ungrammatical period which, if it were to stand, might suggest Martius is somewhat overcome: Qq/F2/most modern texts set a comma

N [11] F2/most modern texts = 'Cocytus', the correct spelling of the river ancients held to be the gate-way to Hell: Qq/F1 = 'Ocitus'

'M' hand = bloody

Quintus	Reach me thy hand, that I may helpe thee out,	R 38 - e
430	Or wanting strength to doe thee so much good,	
	I may be pluckt into the swallowing wombe,	
	Of this deepe pit, poore Bassianus grave :	
	I have no strength to plucke thee to the brinke.	

Martius   Nor I no strength to clime without thy help.

Quintus   Thy hand once more, I will not loose againe,
435   Till thou art heere aloft, or I below,
                Thou can'st not come to me, I come to thee.

[Boths [1] fall in]
ENTER THE EMPEROUR, AARON THE MOORE [2]

Saturnine   Along with me, Ile see what hole is heere,
                 And what he is that now is leapt into it.

                 Say, who art thou that lately did'st descend,
440   Into this gaping hollow of the earth?

Martius   The unhappie sonne [3] of old Andronicus,
                 Brought hither in a most unluckie houre,
                 To finde thy brother Bassianus dead.

Saturnine   My brother dead?
445   I know thou dost but jest,
                 He and his Lady both are at the Lodge,
                 Upon the North-side of this pleasant Chase,
                 'Tis not an houre since I left him [4] there.

Martius   We know not where you left him all alive,
450   But out alas, heere have we found him dead.

ENTER TAMORA, ANDRONICUS, AND LUCIUS

Tamora   Where is my Lord the King?

Saturnine as
•King• [5]   Heere Tamora, though griev'd [6] with killing griefe.

Tamora   Where is thy brother Bassianus?

R 38 - e / L 39 - e : 2. 3. 237 - 261

[W] [1] F1 - 2 = 'Boths', F3/most modern texts = 'Both'

[SD] [2] some modern texts suggest they are accompanied by Attendants, others have the Attendants enter with Tamora in thirteen lines time

[W] [3] since both sons are now in the pit, most modern texts set Q1's 'sonnes', Q2 - 3/Ff = 'sonne'

[W] [4] in both this and the next line, Qq/most modern texts = 'them', Ff = 'him'

[P] [5] as Tamora's mode of address ('my Lord the King') gives Saturnine the clue how to conduct himself, so the Qq/Ff prefix shifts from 'Saturnine' to 'King'

[W] [6] Qq/Ff/most modern texts = 'griev'd', one modern gloss = 'grip'd', while one text sets 'gride'

King	Now to the bottome dost thou search my wound,
455	Poore Bassianus heere lies murthered.
Tamora	Then all too late I bring this fatall writ,
	The complot of this timelesse Tragedie,
	And wonder greatly that mans face can fold,
	In pleasing smiles such murderous Tyrannie.

[She giveth Saturnine a Letter]

SATURNINUS READS THE LETTER

460 *And if we misse to meete him hansomely,*
Sweet huntsman, Bassianus 'tis we meane,
Doe thou so much as dig the grave for him,
Thou know'st our meaning, looke for thy reward
Among the Nettles at the Elder tree :
465 *Which over-shades the mouth of that same pit :*
Where we decreed to bury Bassianuss
Doe this and purchase us thy lasting friends.

King	Oh Tamora, was ever heard the like?
	This is the pit, and this the Elder tree,
470	Looke sirs, if you can finde the hunts-man out,
	That should have murthered Bassianus heere.
Aaron	My gracious Lord heere is the bag of Gold.
King	¹ Two of thy whelpes, fell Curs of bloody kind
	Have heere bereft my brother of his life :
475	Sirs drag them from the pit unto the prison,
	There let them bide untill we have devis'd
	Some never heard-of tortering paine for them.
Tamora	What are they in this pit, →²
	Oh wondrous thing!
480	How easily murder is discovered? ³
Titus	⁴ High Emperour, upon my feeble knee,

L 39 - e : 2. 3. 262 - 288

WHO ₁ most modern texts suggest this is spoken to Titus

SP ₂ the minute pauses inherent in this Ff only pair of short lines (6/4/ syllables) allow a wonderful moment of play-acted emotion (shock? horror?): most modern texts follow Qq and set the two lines as one

SD ₃ at least one modern text suggests the Attendants now pull Bassianus' body and Titus' two sons from out of the pit, though such an activity would seriously detract from the all important on-stage action: other modern texts are reticent as to when the pit-emptying could take place even though Qq/Ff's dialogue (lines 497, next page) suggests it occur at the end of the scene (which would magnificently counterpoise the entry of the ravished and mutilated Lavinia)

SD ₄ most modern texts indicate Titus now kneels

		I beg[†1] this boone, with teares, not lightly shed,	
		That this fell fault of my accursed Sonnes,	
		Accursed, if the faults [2] be prov'd in them. [3]	
485	King	If it be prov'd? you see it is apparant,	L 39 - e
		Who found this Letter, Tamora was it you?	
	Tamora	Andronicus himselfe did take it up.	
	Titus	I did my Lord, →[4]	
		Yet let me be their baile,	
490		For by my Fathers reverent [5] Tombe I vow	
		They shall be ready at your Highnes will,	
		To answere their suspition with their lives.	
	King	Thou shalt not baile them, see thou follow me:	
		Some bring the murthered body, some the murtherers,	
495		Let them not speake a word, the guilt is plaine,	
		For by my soule, were there worse end then death,	
		That end upon them should be executed. [6]	
	Tamora	Andronicus I will entreat the King,	
		Feare not thy Sonnes, they shall do well enough.	
500	Titus	Come Lucius come, →[7]	
		Stay not to talke with them.	

[Exeunt]
ENTER THE EMPRESSE SONNES, WITH LAVINIA, HER HANDS CUT OFF AND
HER TONGUE CUT OUT, AND RAVISHT
[Most modern texts create a new scene here, Act Two Scene 4]

	Demetrius	So now goe tell and if thy tongue can speake,
		Who t'was that cut thy tongue and ravisht thee.
	Chiron	Write downe thy mind, bewray thy meaning so,
505		And if thy stumpes will let thee play the Scribe.

[W][1] F2/most modern texts = 'I beg', F1 = 'Ibeg'

[W][2] Qq/Ff = 'faults', most modern texts set the singular 'fault'

[PCT][3] most modern texts set a dash as if the King interrupts him: Qq/Ff set a period

[SP][4] the pair of Ff only short lines (4/6 syllables) suggest Titus needs a moment to try to deal with the situation: most modern texts follow Qq and set the two lines as one

[W][5] F4/most modern texts = 'reverend', Qq/F1 - 3 = 'reverent'

[SD][6] some modern texts suggest Saturnine and his Attendants now leave, ensuring Tamora's speech to Titus will not be overheard

[SP][7] the minute pauses in the Ff only two short lines (4/6 or 7 syllables) succinctly set up Titus' struggle for self-control: most modern texts follow Qq and set the two lines as one

Demetrius	See how with signes and tokens she can scowle. [1]
Chiron	Goe home, → [2] Call for sweet water, wash thy hands.
Demetrius	She hath no tongue to call, nor hands to wash.
510	And so let's leave her to her silent walkes.
Chiron	And t'were my cause, I should goe hang my selfe. *– feel bad?*
Demetrius	If thou had'st hands to helpe thee knit the cord. *chiron pull'D away*

[Exeunt]
WINDE HORNES.
ENTER MARCUS FROM HUNTING, TO LAVINIA

Who is this, my Neece that flies away so fast?
Cosen a word, where is your husband? *– sees*
515 If I do dreame, would all my wealth would wake me;
If I doe wake, some Planet strike me downe,
That I may slumber in [3] eternall sleepe.
Speake gentle Neece, what sterne ungentle hands
Hath lopt, and hew'd, and made thy body bare
520 Of her two branches, those sweet Ornaments
Whose circkling shadowes, Kings have sought to sleep in
And might not gaine so great a happines
As halfe thy Love: Why doost not speake to me?
Alas, a Crimson river of warme blood, *– Mouth*
525 Like to a bubling fountaine stir'd with winde,
Doth rise and fall betweene thy Rosed lips,
Comming and going with thy hony breath.
But sure some Tereus hath defloured thee,
And least thou should'st detect them,[4] cut thy tongue.
530 Ah, now thou turn'st away thy face for shame:
And notwithstanding all this losse of blood,
As from a Conduit with their [5] issuing Spouts,
Yet doe thy cheekes look red as Titans face,
Blushing to be encountred with a Cloud,
535 Shall I speake for thee? shall I say 'tis so?

[W1] Qq/Ff = 'scrowl/scrowle' which most modern texts set as 'scrawl'

[SP2] the hesitation implied in the Ff only two short lines (2/8 syllables) underlines the impossibility of Lavinia ever truly returning home, hence whatever (possible non-) response which gives rise to Chiron's second short line

[W3] Q1/most modern texts = 'an', Q2 - 3/Ff = 'in'

[W4] though Qq/Ff set 'them', most modern texts set the gloss 'him'

[W5] though Qq/Ff set 'their', most modern texts set the gloss 'three'

Oh that I knew thy hart, and knew the beast
That I might raile at him to ease my mind.

Sorrow concealed, like an Oven stopt,
Doth burne the hart to Cinders where it is.

540   Faire Philomela [1] she but lost her tongue,
And in a tedious Sampler sowed her minde.

But lovely Neece, that meane is cut from thee,
A craftier Tereus [2] hast thou met withall,
And he hath cut those pretty fingers[†3] off,   R 39 - e
545   That could have better sowed then Philomel.
Oh had the monster seene those Lilly hands,
Tremble like Aspen leaves upon a Lute,
And make the silken strings delight to kisse them,
He would not then have toucht them for his life.

550   Or had he heard the heavenly Harmony,
Which[†4] that sweet tongue hath made :
He would have dropt his knife and fell asleepe,
As Cerberus at the Thracian Poets feete.

Come, let us goe, and make thy father blinde,
555   For such a sight will blinde a fathers eye.

One houres storme will drowne the fragrant meades,
What, will whole months of teares thy Fathers eyes?

Doe not draw backe, for we will mourne with thee :
Oh could our mourning ease thy misery.

[Exeunt]

R 39 - e / L 40 - e : 2. 4. 34 - 57

[1] Q1 - 2/most modern texts set 'why' which Q3/Ff omit: some commentators who add 'why' also suggest reducing 'Philomela' to 'Philomel' to preserve the line as pentameter

[2] Q1 - 2/most modern texts add 'Cosen' and omit Ff's 'withall' at the end of the line

[3] F2/most modern texts = 'fingers', F1 = 'fi ngers'

[4] F2/most modern texts = 'Which', F1 = Whic h'

Actus Tertius

**ENTER THE JUDGES AND SENATOURS WITH TITUS TWO SONNES BOUND, [1]
PASSING ON THE STAGE TO THE PLACE OF EXECUTION, AND TITUS GOING
BEFORE PLEADING**

Titus   Heare me grave fathers, noble Tribunes stay,
For pitty of mine age, whose youth was spent
In dangerous warres, whilst you securely slept:
For all my blood in Romes great quarrell shed,
5   For all the frosty nights that I have watcht,
And for these bitter teares, which now you see,
Filling the aged wrinkles in my cheekes,
Be pittifull to my condemned Sonnes,
Whose soules is [2] not corrupted as 'tis thought:
10   For two and twenty sonnes [3] I never wept,
Because they died in honours lofty bed.

*walking
noise gets
louder*

ANDRONICUS LYETH DOWNE, AND THE JUDGES PASSE BY HIM

For these, [4] Tribunes, in the dust I write
My harts deepe languor, and my soules sad teares:
Let my teares stanch the earths drie appetite.

15   My sonnes sweet blood, will make it shame and blush:
O earth! I will be friend [5] thee more with raine

               [Exeunt] [6]

That shall distill from these two ancient ruines, [7]
Then youthfull Aprill shall with all his showres
In summers drought: Ile drop upon thee still,
20   In Winter with warme teares Ile melt the snow,
And keepe eternall†[8] spring time on thy face,
So thou refuse to drinke my deare sonnes blood.

N[1] most modern texts remind readers that the sons are Martius and Quintus

W[2] Qq/F1/most modern texts = 'is', F2 = 'are'

F[3] many commentators point out that earlier (Act One Scene 1, line 203 page 8) Titus claimed 'one and twenty Valiant Sonnes' had been killed in battle: either he is now confused, or has added to the list Mutius, whom he himself killed on-stage

W[4] at least two modern texts have added 'two' to create pentameter: Qq/Ff do not set the word: the original short setting once more suggests Titus is trying to maintain self-control

W[5] F1 - 2 = 'be friend', F3/most modern texts = 'befriend'

SD[6] most modern texts suggest all exit except Titus, sometimes advancing the exit one line

W[7] an often discussed gloss = 'urns', though most texts set Qq/Ff's 'ruines'

W[8] F2/most modern texts = 'eternall', F1 = 'erernall'

ENTER LUCIUS, WITH HIS WEAPON DRAWNE

Oh reverent [1] Tribunes, oh gentle aged men,
Unbinde my sonnes, reverse the doome of death,
25 And let me say (that never wept before)
My [12] teares are now prevaling [3] Oratours.

Lucius
Oh noble father, you lament in vaine,
The Tribunes heare [4] not, no man is by,
And you recount your sorrowes to a stone.

30 Titus
Ah Lucius for thy brothers let me plead,
Grave Tribunes, once more I intreat of you.

Lucius
My gracious Lord, no Tribune heares you speake.

Titus
Why 'tis no matter man, if they did heare
They would not marke me: oh if they did heare
35 They would not pitty me. [5] *unavailing*
Therefore I tell my sorrowes bootles to the stones. [6] | L 40 - e

Who though they cannot answere my distresse,
Yet in some sort they are better then the Tribunes,
For that they will not intercept my tale;
40 When I doe weepe, they humbly at my feete
Receive my teares, and seeme to weepe with me,
And were they but attired in grave weedes,
Rome could afford no Tribune like to these.
A stone is as soft [7] waxe, → [8]

L 40 - e / R 40 - e : 3. 1. 23 - 45

[1] F3/most modern texts = 'reverend', Qq/F1 - 2 = 'reverent'

[2] F2/most modern texts = 'My', F1 = 'M y'

[3] Qq/F3/most modern texts = 'prevailing', F1 - 2 = 'prevaling'

[4] Qq/F2 - 4/most modern texts set 'you', which F1 omits (F1 thus sets a nine syllable line)

ADD/LS [5] Qq and most modern texts set the following
They would not marke me, if they did marke
They would not pittie me, yet pleade I must
And bootlesse unto them.
Therefore I tell my sorrowes to the stones.
with *The Oxford Shakespeares*, ops. cit., omitting the last line: Ff set a shorter passage viz.
They would not marke me: oh if they did heare
They would not pitty me.
Therefore I tell my sorrowes bootles to the stones.

PCT [6] F1 sets a period, as if the following brand new realisation forces Titus to a complete stop: Qq/F3/most modern texts set a comma

[7] Qq/most modern texts = 'soft as', Ff = 'as soft'

SP [8] this is the first of five pairs of Ff only short lines to be found in the right hand column of page #40 of the Tragedy section which Qq/most modern texts set as five single lines: here, if the hesitations of the Ff reading were to stand (6/6 syllables) they might suggest Titus struggling to, and succeeding in, maintaining self-control: Qq/modern texts setting an onrushing twelve syllable line suggests exactly the opposite

41

45	Tribunes more hard then stones:
	A stone is silent, and offendeth not,
	And Tribunes with their tongues doome men to death.
	But wherefore stand'st thou with thy weapon drawne?

Lucius   To rescue my two brothers from their death,
50   For which attempt the Judges have pronounc'st
My everlasting doome of banishment.

Titus   O happy man, they have befriended thee:
Why foolish Lucius, dost thou not perceive
That Rome is but a wildernes of Tigers?

55   Tigers must pray, and Rome affords no prey
But me and and [1] mine: how happy art thou then,
From these devourers to be banished?

But who comes with our brother Marcus heere?

ENTER MARCUS AND LAVINIA

Marcus   Titus, prepare thy noble [2] eyes to weepe,
60   Or if not so, thy noble heart to breake:
I bring consuming sorrow to thine age.

Titus   Will it consume me?
    Let me see it then.

Marcus	This was thy daughter.
Titus	Why Marcus so she is.
Lucius	Aye me this object kils me. [3]

Titus   Faint-harted boy, arise and looke upon her,
Speake Lavinia, what accursed hand
Hath made thee handlesse in thy Fathers sight?

70   What foole hath added water to the Sea?
Or brought a faggot to bright burning Troy?

My griefe was at the height before thou cam'st,
And now like Nylus it disdaineth bounds:

W [1] Qq/F2/most modern texts = 'and', F1 = 'and and'

W [2] Q1 - 2/most modern texts = 'aged', Q3/Ff = 'noble'

LS [3] the actor has choice as to which two of these three short lines may be joined as one line of split verse

Give me a sword, Ile chop off my hands too,
75   For they have fought for Rome, and all in vaine :
And they have nur'st this woe, → [1]
In feeding life :
In bootelesse prayer have they bene held up,
And they have serv'd me to effectlesse use.

80   Now all the service I require of them,
Is that the one will helpe to cut the other :
'Tis well Lavinia, that thou hast no hands,
For hands to do Rome service is but vaine.

Lucius   Speake gentle sister, who hath martyr'd thee?

85   **Marcus**   O that delightfull engine of her thoughts,
That blab'd them with such pleasing eloquence,
Is torne from forth that pretty hollow cage,
Where like a sweet mellodius bird it sung,
Sweet varied notes inchanting every eare.

90   **Lucius**   Oh say thou for her, → [2]
Who hath done this deed?

Marcus   Oh thus I found her straying in the Parke,
Seeking to hide herselfe as doth the Deare
That hath receivde some unrecuring wound.

95   **Titus**   It was my Deare, → [3]
And he that wounded her,
Hath hurt me more, then had he kild me dead :
For now I stand as one upon a Rocke,
Inviron'd with a wildernesse of Sea.

100   Who markes the waxing tide, → [4]
Grow wave by wave,   R 40 - e
Expecting ever when some envious surge,
Will in his brinish bowels swallow him.

This way to death my wretched sonnes are gone :
105   Heere stands my other sonne, a banisht man,
And heere my brother weeping at my woes.

R 40 - e / L 41 - e : 3. 1. 72 - 100

SP[1] the Ff only two short lines (6/4 syllables) could once more mark a moment where Titus is fighting for self-control: most modern texts follow Qq and set the two lines as one

SP[2] as seen throughout the text so far, most of the Ff only short lines seem to suggest Titus is fighting for self-control: here the two short lines (5/5 syllables) show Lucius in the same state: most modern texts follow Qq and set the two lines as one, as they do with the next two pairs (4/6 and 6/4 syllables)

SP[3] see footnote #2 above

SP[4] ditto

But that which gives my soule the greatest spurne,
Is deere Lavinia, deerer then my soule.

Had I but seene thy picture in this plight,
110   It would have madded me.
                  What shall I doe?
Now I behold thy lively body so?

Thou hast no hands to wipe away thy teares,
Nor tongue to tell me who hath martyr'd thee:
115   Thy husband he is dead, and for his death
Thy brothers are condemn'd, and dead by this.

Looke Marcus, ah sonne Lucius looke on her:
When I did name her brothers, then fresh teares
Stood on her cheekes, as doth the hony dew,
120   Upon a gathred Lillie almost withered. [+1]

Marcus   Perchance she weepes because they kil'd her
              husband,
Perchance because she knowes him [2] innocent.

Titus   If they did kill thy husband then be joyfull,
125   Because the law hath tane revenge on them.   B ro's

No, no, they would not doe so foule a deede, ⚡
Witnes the sorrow that their sister makes.

Gentle Lavinia let me kisse thy lips,
Or make some signes [3] how I may do thee ease: 10
130   Shall thy good Uncle, and thy [+4] brother Lucius, 11
And thou and I sit round about some Fountaine, 11
Looking all downewards to behold our cheekes 9
How they are stain'd in [5] meadowes, yet not dry 10
With miery slime left on them by a flood: ⌃   miery = Mud
135   And in the Fountaine shall we gaze so long,
Till the fresh taste be taken from that cleerenes,
And made a brine pit with our bitter teares?

Or shall we cut away our hands like thine?

Or shall we bite our tongues, and in dumbe shewes
140   Passe the remainder of our hatefull dayes?

L 41 - e : 3. 1. 101 - 132

[PCT 1] F1 sets the strange ending punctuation of a period immediately followed by a comma: F2 sets a comma,
     Qq/F3/most modern texts set a period
[▼ 2] Q1/most modern texts = 'them', Q2 - 3/Ff = 'him'
[▼ 3] Qq/most modern texts = 'signe', Ff = 'signes'
[▼ 4] F2/most modern texts = 'and thy', F1 = 'andthy'
[▼/PCT 5] Q1/most modern texts = ', like'; Q2 - 3/Ff = 'in', with no preceding punctuation

What shall we doe?
        Let us that have our tongues
Plot some devise of further miseries [1]
To make us wondred at in time to come.

145 **Lucius**   Sweet Father cease your teares, for at your griefe
See how my wretched sister sobs and weeps.

Marcus   Patience deere Neece, good Titus drie thine
eyes.

Titus   Ah Marcus, Marcus, Brother well I wot, ᴷⁱˢᵉʷ
150 Thy napkin cannot drinke a teare of mine,
For thou poore man hast drown'd it with thine owne.

Lucius   Ah my Lavinia I will wipe thy cheekes.

Titus   Marke Marcus marke, I understand her signes,
Had she a tongue to speake, now would she say
155 That to her brother which I said to thee.

His Napkin with her [2] true teares all bewet,
Can do no service on her sorrowfull cheekes.

Oh what a simpathy of woe is this!
As farre from helpe as Limbo is from blisse,[3]

ENTER ARON THE MOORE ALONE

160 **Moore**   Titus Andronicus, my Lord the Emperour,
Sends thee this word, that if thou love thy sonnes,
Let Marcus, Lucius, or thy selfe old Titus,
Or any one of you, chop off your hand,
And send it to the King: he for the same,
165 Will send thee hither both thy sonnes alive,
And that shall be the ransome for their fault.   L 41 - e

Titus   Oh gracious Emperour, oh gentle Aaron.
Did ever Raven sing so like a Larke,
That gives sweet tydings of the Sunnes uprise?
170 With all my heart, Ile send the Emperour my hand,
Good Aron wilt thou help to chop it off?

L 41 - e / R 41 - e : 3. 1. 133 - 161

[1] Qq/most modern texts = 'miserie', Ff = 'miseries'

[2] F4/most modern texts = 'his', Qq/F1 - 3 = 'her', also F1 sets 'hertrue', while other texts separate 'true' from
the previous word

[3] F1 sets a comma, as if Aaron's entry interrupts Titus : Qq/F2/most modern texts set a period

Lucius	Stay Father, for that noble hand of thine,
	That hath throwne downe so many enemies,
	Shall not be sent: my hand will serve the turne,
175	My youth can better spare my blood then you,
	And therfore mine shall save my brothers lives.
Marcus	Which of your hands hath not defended Rome,
	And rear'd aloft the bloody Battleaxe,
	Writing destruction on the enemies Castle?
180	Oh none of both but are of high desert:
	My hand hath bin but idle, let it serve
	To ransome my two nephewes from their death,
	Then have I kept it to a worthy end.
Moore	Nay come agree, whose hand shall goe[†1] along
185	For feare they die before their pardon come.
Marcus	My hand shall goe.
Lucius	By heaven it shall not goe.
Titus	Sirs strive no more, such withered hearbs as these
	Are meete for plucking up, and therefore mine.
190 Lucius	Sweet Father, if I shall be thought thy sonne,
	Let me redeeme my brothers both from death.
Marcus	And for our fathers sake, and mothers care,
	Now let me shew a brothers love to thee.
Titus	Agree betweene you, I will spare my hand.
195 Lucius	Then Ile goe fetch an Axe.
Marcus	But I will use the Axe.

[Exeunt] [2]

Titus	Come hither Aaron, Ile deceive them both,
	Lend me thy hand, and I will give thee mine,[3]
Moore	[4] If that be cal'd deceit, I will be honest,
200	And never whilst I live deceive men so:
	But Ile deceive you in another sort,
	And that you'l say ere halfe an houre passe.

R 41 - e : 3. 1. 162 - 191

[W 1] F2/most modern texts = 'shall goe', F1 = 'shallgoe'

[SD 2] most modern texts explain Titus and Aaron stay behind

[PCT 3] F1 - 2 set a comma, as if Titus immediately moves into preparing himself for the removal of his hand: Qq/F3/most modern texts set a period

[A 4] most modern texts suggest the rest of this speech is spoken as an aside

HE CUTS OFF TITUS HAND

ENTER LUCIUS AND MARCUS AGAINE †1

Titus	Now stay you ² strife, what shall be, is dispatcht :
	Good Aron give his Majestie me ³ hand,
205	Tell him, it was a hand that warded him
	From thousand dangers : bid him bury it :
	More hath it merited : That let it have.
	As for for ⁴ my sonnes, say I account of them,
	As jewels purchast at an easie price,
210	And yet deere too, because I bought mine owne.
Aaron	I goe Andronicus, and for thy hand,
	Looke by and by to have thy sonnes with thee :
⁵	Their heads I meane : Oh how this villany
	Doth fat me with the very thoughts of it.
215	Let fooles doe good, and faire men call for grace,
	Aron will have his soule blacke like his face.

[Exit]

Titus	⁶ O heere I lift this one hand up to heaven,
	And bow this feeble ruine to the earth,
	If any power pitties wretched teares,
220	To that I call : ⁷ what wilt thou kneele with me?
	Doe then deare heart, for heaven shall heare our prayers,
	Or with our sighs weele breath the welkin dimme, *sky = welkin*
	And staine the Sun with fogge as somtime†⁸ cloudes,
	When they do hug him in their melting bosomes.
225 **Marcus**	Oh brother speake with possibilities,⁹
	And do not breake into these deepe extreames.
Titus	Is not my sorrow deepe, having no bottome? R 41 - e
	Then be my passions bottomlesse with them.

R 41 - e / L 42 - e : 3. 1. 192 - 217

ᵂ₁ F2/most modern texts = 'Marcus againe', F1 = 'Marcu sAgaine'

ᵂ₂ Qq/F2/most modern texts = 'your', F1 = 'you'

ᵂ₃ Qq/F2/most modern texts = 'my', F1 = 'me'

ᵂ₄ Qq/F2/most modern texts = 'for', F1 = 'for for'

ᴬ₅ most modern texts suggest the rest of the speech is spoken as an aside

ˢᴰ₆ most modern texts suggest Titus kneels

ˢᴰ/ᵂ₇ most modern texts suggest Lavinia now kneels with him, also setting Q1's 'wouldst' rather than Ff's 'wilt' (Q2 - 3 = 'would')

ᵂ₈ F2 = 'as sometime', F1 = 'a ssomtime'

ᵂ₉ Q1 - 2/most modern texts = 'possibilitie', Q3/Ff = 'possibilities'

Marcus	But yet let reason governe thy lament.

230 **Titus**

> If there were reason for these miseries,
> Then into limits could I binde my woes:
> When heaven doth weepe, doth not the earth oreflow?
> If the windes rage, doth not the Sea wax mad,
> Threatning the welkin with his big-swolne face?
> 235 And wilt thou have a reason for this coile? [1]

I am the Sea.
        Harke how her sighes doe [2] flow:
Shee is the weeping welkin, I the earth:
Then must my Sea be moved with her sighes,
240 Then must my earth with her continuall teares,
Become a deluge: overflow'd and drown'd:
For why, my bowels cannot hide her woes,
But like a drunkard must I vomit them:
Then give me leave, for loosers will have leave,
245 To ease their stomackes with their bitter tongues,[3]

ENTER A MESSENGER WITH TWO HEADS AND A HAND

Messenger   Worthy Andronicus, ill art thou repaid,
For that good hand thou sentst the Emperour:
Heere are the heads of thy two noble sonnes.

And heeres thy hand in scorne to thee sent backe:
250 Thy griefes,[4] their sports: Thy resolution mockt,
That woe is me to thinke upon thy woes,
More then remembrance of my fathers death.

[Exit]

Marcus   Now let hot Ætna coole in Cicilie,
And be my heart an ever-burning hell:
255 These miseries are more then may be borne.

To weepe with them that weepe, doth ease some deale,
But sorrow flouted at, is double death.

Lucius   Ah that this sight should make so deep a wound,
And yet detested life not shrinke thereat:
260 That ever death should let life beare his name,
Where life hath no more interest but to breath.

ᵗˢᵀ[1] this passage could be set as any where between one and three sentences

ᵂ[2] Q1/most modern texts = 'doth', Q2-3/Ff = 'doe'

ᴾᶜᵀ[3] F1 - 2 set a comma, as if the Messenger interrupts Titus: Qq/F3/most modern texts set a period

ᵂ[4] Q1/most modern texts = 'griefe', Q2 - 3/Ff = 'griefes'

Marcus	[1]	Alas poore hart that kisse is comfortlesse,
		As frozen water to a starved snake.

Titus   When will this fearefull slumber have an end?

265   **Marcus**   Now farwell flatterie, die Andronicus,
Thou dost not slumber, see thy two sons heads,
Thy warlike hands,[2] thy mangled daughter here:
Thy other banisht sonnes [3] with this deere sight
Strucke pale and bloodlesse, and thy brother I,
270   Even like a stony Image, cold and numme.

Ah now no more will I controule my [4] griefes,
Rent off thy silver haire, thy other hand
Gnawing with thy teeth, and be this dismall sight
The closing up of our most wretched eyes:
275   Now is a time to storme, why art thou still?

Titus   Ha, ha, ha,[5]

Marcus   Why dost thou laugh? it fits not with this houre.

Titus   Why I have not another teare to shed:
Besides, this sorrow is an enemy,
280   And would usurpe upon my watry eyes,
And make them blinde with tributarie teares.

Then which way shall I finde Revenges Cave?
For these two heads doe seeme to speake to me,
And threat me, I shall never come to blisse,
285   Till all these mischiefes be returned againe,
Even in their throats that have [6] committed them.

Come let me see what taske I have to doe,
You heavie people, circle me about,
That I may turne me to each one of you,
290   And sweare unto my soule to right your wrongs.

The vow is made, come Brother take a head,   L 42 - e
And in this hand the other will I beare. [7]

L 42 - e / R 42 - e : 3. 1. 250 - 280

SD [1] most modern texts suggest Lavinia kisses Titus, thus occasioning Marcus' comment

▼ [2] Qq/F4/most modern texts = 'hand', F1 - 3 = 'hands'

▼ [3] Qq/F4/most modern texts = 'Son', F1 - 3 = 'sonnes'

▼ [4] Q1/most modern texts = 'thy', Q2 - 3/Ff = 'my'

PCT [5] F1 sets a comma as if Marcus interrupts him: Qq/F2/most modern texts set a period

▼ [6] Q1/most modern texts = 'hath', Q2 - 3/Ff = 'have'

▼ [7] F1 - 3 set a period, perhaps suggesting something moves Titus to include Lavinia (first line, next page) in the ritual of the exit: Qq/F4/most modern texts set a period

And Lavinia thou shalt be employd in these things: ¹
Beare thou my hand sweet wench betweene thy teeth: ²
295   As for thee boy, goe get thee from my sight,
Thou art an Exile, and thou must not stay,
Hie to the Gothes, and raise an army there,
And if *you love me, as I thinke you doe,
Let's kisse and part, for we have much to doe.

[Exeunt]
MANET LUCIUS

300   **Lucius**   Farewell Andronicus my noble Father:
The woful'st man that ever liv'd in Rome:
Farewell proud Rome, til Lucius come againe,
He loves †³ his pledges dearer then his life:
Farewell Lavinia my noble sister,
305   O would thou wert as thou to fore hast beene,
But now, not Lucius nor Lavinia lives
But in oblivion and hateful griefes:
If Lucius live, he will requit your wrongs,
And make proud Saturnine and his Empresse
310   Beg at the gates likes ⁴ Tarquin and his Queene.

Now will I to the Gothes and raise a power,
To be reveng'd on Rome and Saturnine.

[Exit Lucius]
A BANKET †⁵
ENTER ANDRONICUS, MARCUS, LAVINIA, AND THE BOY ⁶
[Most modern texts create a new scene here, Act Three Scene 2] ⁷

Tjtus as
•**Andronicus**•   So, so, now sit, and looke you eate no more
Then will preserve just so much strength in us
315   As will revenge these bitter woes of ours.

▼ ¹
  Qq set 'in these Armes', Ff = 'in these things': several modern texts omit the phrase: for further details see
The Arden Shakespeare, Titus Andronicus, op. cit., page 201, footnote to lines 282 - 3

▼ ²
  Qq/Ff/most modern texts set 'teeth': *The Oxford Shakespeare,* op cit., substitutes 'Armes' from Qq's previous
line

▼ ³
  Qq/Ff/most modern texts = 'loves', one gloss = 'leaves', also F3/most modern texts = 'He loves', F1 - 2 sets
'Heloves'

▼ ⁴
  Qq/F2/most modern texts = 'like', F1 = 'likes'

SD ⁵
  F1 = 'Bnaket', the correct setting of which, 'Banket', suggests a light meal: F2/some modern texts reset this as
the more formal 'banquet' (see also the following footnote)

SD ⁶
  most modern texts name the Boy as Young Lucius, taking the name from the opening stage direction of Act
Four Scene 1: also, some modern texts add Attendants (with this, and the enlarging of the 'banket' to a
'banquet' - see the preceding footnote - there is the danger of turning the scene into something larger and more
grandiose than might have been first intended)

F/LS ⁷
  this scene is set in Ff/most modern texts only: for further details, see the specific Introduction to this play

Marcus unknit that sorrow-wreathen knot:
Thy Neece and I (poore Creatures) want our hands
And cannot passionate our tenfold griefe,
With foulded Armes.
320   This poore right hand of mine,
Is left to tirranize uppon my breast. [1]

Who when my hart all mad with misery,
Beats in this hollow prison of my flesh,
Then thus I thumpe it downe.
325   [2] Thou Map of woe, that thus dost talke in signes,
When thy poore hart beates without ragious [3] beating,
Thou canst not strike it thus to make it still?

Wound it with sighing girle, kil it with grones:
Or get some little knife betweene thy teeth,
330 And just against thy hart make thou a hole,
That all the teares that thy poore eyes let fall
May run into that sinke, and soaking in,
Drowne the lamenting foole, in Sea salt teares.

Marcus   Fy brother fy, teach her not thus to lay
335   Such violent hands uppon her tender life.

Andronicus   How now!
        Has sorrow made thee doate already?
Why Marcus, no man should be mad but I:
What violent hands can she lay on her life:
340 Ah, wherefore dost thou urge the name of hands,
To bid Æneas tell the tale twice ore
How Troy was burnt, and he made miserable?

O handle not the theame, to talke of hands,
Least we remember still that we have none,
345 Fie, fie, how Frantiquely I square my talke
As if we should forget we had no hands:
If Marcus did not name the word of hands.

Come, lets fall too, and gentle girle eate this,
Heere is no drinke?
350   Harke Marcus what she saies,
I can interpret all her martir'd signes,
She saies, she drinkes no other drinke but teares

---

[1] F1 sets a period, perhaps suggesting Titus needs a moment to establish some form of control; F2 sets no punctuation, while most modern texts set a comma

[2] most modern texts indicate this is said to Lavinia

[3] F2/most modern texts = 'with outragious', F1 = 'without ragious'

Breu'd with her sorrow: mesh'd [1] uppon her cheekes,   R 42 - e
Speechlesse complaynet, I [2] will learne thy thought:
355   In thy dumb action, will I be as perfect
As begging Hermits in their holy prayers.

Thou shalt not sighe nor hold thy stumps to heaven,
Nor winke, nor nod, nor kneele, nor make a signe,
But I (of these) will wrest an Alphabet,
360   And by still practice, learne to know thy meaning.

Boy   Good grandsire leave these bitter deepe laments,
Make my Aunt merry, with some pleasing tale.

Marcus   Alas, the tender boy in passion mov'd,
Doth weepe to see his grandsires heavinesse.

365   **Andronicus**   Peace tender Sapling, thou art made of teares,
And teares will quickly melt thy life away.

MARCUS STRIKES THE DISH WITH A KNIFE

What doest thou strike at Marcus with [3] knife.

Marcus   At that that I have kil'd my Lord, a Flys [4]

Andronicus   Out on the murderour: thou kil'st my hart,
370   Mine eyes [5] cloi'd with view of Tirranie:
A deed of death done on the Innocent
Becoms not Titus brother: †[6] get thee gone,
I see thou art not for my company.

Marcus   Alas (my Lord) I have but kild a flie.

375   **Andronicus**   But?
        How: if that Flie had a father and mother?

How would he hang his slender gilded wings
And buz lamenting doings [7] in the ayer,
Poore harmelesse Fly,
380   That with his pretty buzing melody,

---

[1] Ff = 'mesh'd', most modern texts set 'mashed'

[2] F1 = 'complaynet, I will', F2 - 4 = 'complaint, O I will': most modern texts = 'complainer, I'

[3] F2 - 4/most modern texts add 'thy', setting a ten syllable line: F1 omits the word

[4] F1 = 'Flys' with no final punctuation: F2 - 4/most modern texts = 'Fly' followed by a period

[5] F2 - 4/most modern texts add 'are', creating a ten syllable line: F1 omits the word

[6] F2/most modern texts = 'brother', F1 = 'broher'

[7] Ff = 'doings', modern glosses include 'dolings' and 'dirges'

	Came heere to make us merry, → And thou hast kil'd him.
Marcus	Pardon me sir, → It was a blacke illfavour'd Fly, [1]
385	Like to the Empresse Moore, therefore I kild him.

Andronicus	O, o, o,
	Then pardon me for reprehending thee,
	For thou hast done a Charitable deed:
	Give me thy knife, I will insult on him,
390	Flattering my selfes, [2] as if it were the Moore,
	Come hither purposely to poyson me.

– Idea for Revenge from #14

There's for thy selfe, and thats for Tamira: ° Ah sirra, °[3]
Yet I thinke we are not brought so low,
But that betweene us, we can kill a Fly,

395	That comes in likenesse of a Cole-blacke Moore.

Marcus	Alas poore man, griefe ha's so wrought on him,
	He takes false shadowes, for true substances.

Andronicus	Come, take away: Lavinia, goe with me,
	Ile to thy closset, and goe read with thee
400	Sad stories, chanced in the times of old.
	Come boy, and goe with me, thy sight is young,
	And thou shalt read, when mine begin to dazell.

[Exeunt]

LS 1 Ff set four short lines (7/5/4/8), the hesitations perhaps suggesting careful self-control between the two men: most modern texts set two on-rushing twelve syllable lines as shown: see the next footnote but one

W 2 Qq/F2/most modern texts = 'selfe', F1 = 'selfes'

LS 3 surprisingly, considering most modern texts have joined most Ff paired short lines - often creating lines longer than ten syllables - here, when Ff set a thirteen syllable line showing Titus snapping at last, some modern texts split the line in two (10/3 syllables) - creating normality and a pause when a blurt was originally set

Actus Quartus

ENTER YOUNG LUCIUS AND LAVINIA RUNNING ^{†1} AFTER HIM, AND
THE BOY FLIES FROM HER WITH HIS BOOKES UNDER HIS ARME.
ENTER TITUS AND MARCUS

Boy	Helpe Grandsier helpe, my Aunt Lavinia,	
	Followes me every where I know not why.	
	Good Uncle Marcus see how swift she comes,	
	Alas sweet Aunt, I know not what you meane.	
5 Marcus	Stand by me Lucius, doe not feare *thy Aunt.	
˙Titus˙	She loves thee boy too well to doe thee harme ²	
Boy	I when my father was in Rome she did.	L 43 - e
Marcus	What meanes my Neece Lavinia by these signes?	
Titus	Feare ³ not Lucius, somewhat doth she meane:	
10	⁴ See Lucius see, how much she makes of thee:	
	Some whether would she have thee goe with her.	
	Ah boy, Cornelia never with more care	
	Read to her sonnes, then she hath read to thee,	
	Sweet Poetry, and Tullies Oratour:	
15	Canst thou not gesse wherefore she plies thee thus?	
Boy	My Lord I know not I, nor can I gesse,	
	Unlesse some fit or frenzie do possesse her:	
	For I have heard my Grandsier say full oft,	
	Extremitie of griefes would make men mad.	
20	And I have read that Hecubæ ⁵ of Troy,	
	Ran mad through ⁶ sorrow, that made me to feare,	
	Although my Lord, I know my noble Aunt,	
	Loves me as deare as ere my mother did,	
	And would not but in fury fright my youth,	

L 43 - e / R 43 - e : 4. 1. 1 - 24

^{SD}₁ F2/most modern texts = 'Lavinia Running', F1 = 'LaviniaRunning'

^{PCT}₂ F1 - 2 set no punctuation, as if the Boy interrupts him: Qq/F3/most modern texts set a period

^W₃ though the pronouncing of 'Lucius' as trisyllabic ('Lu-ci-us') would establish a ten-syllable line, most modern texts do so by adding 'her' from Qq, which Ff omit

^{P/LS}₄ though Qq/Ff set these lines as the continuation of Titus' speech, most modern texts assign them to Marcus

^N₅ Qq/F2/most modern texts set the more recogniseable correct 'Hecuba', F1 = 'Hecubæ'

^W₆ Q1 - 2/most modern texts = 'for', Q3/Ff = 'through'

25	Which made me downe to throw my bookes, and flie Causles perhaps, but pardon me sweet Aunt, And Madam, if my Uncle Marcus goe, I will most willingly attend your Ladyship.
Marcus	Lucius I will.
30 **Titus**	How now Lavinia, Marcus what meanes this? Some booke there is that she desires to see, Which is it girle of these? Open them boy, [1] But thou art deeper read and better skild,
35	Come and take choyse of all my Library, And so beguile thy sorrow, till the heavens Reveale the damn'd contriver of this deed. What booke? [2] Why lifts she up her armes in sequence thus?
40 **Marcus**	I thinke she meanes that ther was [3] more then one Confederate in the fact, I more there was : Or else to heaven she heaves them to [4] revenge.
Titus	Lucius what booke is that she tosseth so?
Boy 45	Grandsier 'tis Ovids Metamorphosis, My mother gave it me.
Marcus	For love of her that's gone, Perhaps†[5] she culd it from among the rest.
Titus	Soft, so busily she turnes the leaves, Helpe her, what would she finde?
50	Lavinia shall I read? This is the tragicke tale of Philomel? And treates of Tereus treason and his rape, And rape I feare was roote of *thine annoy.
Marcus	See brother see, note how she quotes the leaves [6]

WHO [1] most modern texts suggest this is spoken to Lavinia

OM [2] most modern texts omit this Ff only two word phrase, arguing that it merely anticipates Titus' next speech: however, theatrically, the Ff reading has much to offer, allowing a moment of silent desperation for all on-stage as Lavinia still fails to make herself understood

W [3] Q1 - 2/most modern texts = 'were', Q3/Ff = 'was'

W [4] Qq/most modern texts = 'for', Ff = 'to'

W [5] Qq/F2/most modern texts = 'Perhaps', F1 = 'Perhas'

PCT [6] F1 - 2 set no punctuation, as if Titus interrupts him: F3/most modern texts set a period

55	Titus	Lavinia, wert thou thus surpriz'd sweet girle,
		Ravisht and wrong'd as Philomela was?
		Forc'd in the ruthlesse, vast, and gloomy woods?

> See, see,° I such a place there is where we did hunt,° [1]

(O had we never, never hunted there)
60 Patern'd by that the Poet heere describes,
By nature made for murthers and for rapes.

Marcus O why should nature build so foule a den,
Unlesse the Gods delight in tragedies?

Titus Give signes sweet girle, for heere are none but friends
65 What Romaine Lord it was durst do the deed?
Or slunke not Saturnine, as Tarquin ersts,
That left the Campe to sinne in Lucrece bed.

Marcus Sit downe sweet Neece, brother sit downe by me,
Appollo, Pallas, Jove, or Mercury,
70 Inspire me that I may this treason finde.
My Lord looke heere, looke heere Lavinia.

**HE WRITES HIS NAME WITH HIS STAFFE, AND GUIDES IT
WITH FEETE AND MOUTH**

This sandie plot is plaine, guide if thou canst   R 43 - e
This after me, I have [2] writ my name,
Without the helpe of any hand at all.
75 Curst be that hart that forc'st us to that shift:
Write thou good Neece, and heere display at last,
What God will have discovered for revenge,
Heaven guide thy pen to print thy sorrowes plaine,
That we may know the Traytors and the truth.

**SHE TAKES THE STAFFE IN HER MOUTH, AND GUIDES IT WITH HER
STUMPS AND WRITES**

80 Titus   [3] Oh doe ye read my Lord what she hath writs? [4]
Stuprum, Chiron, Demetrius.

LS [1] even though both Qq and Ff set a twelve syllable (onrushed) line, most modern texts set two lines (2/10 syllables) as shown, thus creating a pause where a blurt of excitement (understanding at last?) originally was set

W [2] Qq/Ff set a nine syllable line as shown, allowing a moment's hesitation (as, perhaps, Marcus strives to get Lavinia to participate): some metrically minded modern texts create pentameter by setting either 'I here have' or 'see, I have'

LS/P [3] Q1 - 2 add this to Marcus' following speech, Ff set it for Titus: most modern texts compromise, setting the first line for Marcus, the second for Titus

W [4] Qq/F2/most modern texts = 'writ', F1 = 'writs'

Marcus	What, what, the lustfull sonnes of Tamora, Performers of this hainous bloody deed?
Titus	*Magni Dominator poli,*
85	*Tam lentus†1 audis scelera, tam lentus vides?*
Marcus	Oh calme thee gentle Lord: Although I know There is enough written upon this earth, To stirre a mutinie in the mildest thoughts, And arme the mindes of infants to exclaimes.
90	My Lord kneele downe with me: Lavinia kneele, And kneele sweet boy, the Romaine Hectors hope, And sweare with me, as with the wofull Feere And father of that chast dishonoured Dame, Lord Junius Brutus sweare 2 for Lucrece rape,
95	That we will prosecute (by good advise) Mortall revenge upon these traytorous Gothes, And see their blood, or die with this reproach.
Titus	Tis sure enough, and you knew how. But if you hunt these Beare-whelpes, then beware
100	The Dam will wake, and if she winde *you once, Shee's with the Lyon deepely still in league. And lulls him wilst she palyeth 3 on her backe, And when he sleepes will she do what she list. 4
105	You are a young huntsman Marcus, let it 5 alone: And come, I will goe get a leafe of brasse, And with a Gad of steele will write these words, And lay it by: the angry Northerne winde Will blow these sands like Sibels leaves abroad, And wheres your 6 lesson then.
110	Boy what say you?

W1 Qq/F2/most modern texts = 'lentus', F1 = 'lent us'

W2 Qq/F3/most modern texts = 'swore', F1 - 2 = 'sweare'

W3 Qq/F2/most modern texts = 'playeth', F1 = 'palyeth'

PCT4 as Titus sets up his animal analogy for Tamora, her two sons and Saturnine, Ff's punctuation is somewhat erratic (as is Qq's to a lesser extent), an excellent testament to the emotions churning within: most modern texts rationalise the punctuation along the following lines

> But if you hunt these Beare-whelpes, then beware:
> The Dam will wake, and if she winde you once
> Shee's with the Lyon deepely still in league,
> And lulls him wilst she playeth on her backe,
> And when he sleepes will she do what she list.

setting up a far more in-control character than originally shown

W5 Q3/Ff = 'it', Q1 - 2/most modern texts omit the word

W6 Q1/most modern texts = 'our', Q3/Ff = 'your', Q2 = 'you'

Boy	I say my Lord, that if I were a man,
	Their mothers bed-chamber should not be safe,
	For these bad ¹ bond-men to the yoake of Rome.
Marcus	I that's my boy, thy father hath full oft,
115	For his ungratefull country done the like.
Boy	And Uncle so will I, and if I live.
Titus	Come goe with me into mine Armorie,
	Lucius Ile fit thee, and withall, my boy
	Shall carry from me to the Empresse sonnes,
120	Presents that I intend to send them both,
	Come, come, thou'lt do thy message, wilt thou not?
Boy	I with my dagger in their bosomes Grandsire: ²
Titus	No boy not so, Ile teach thee another course,
	Lavinia come, Marcus looke to my house,
125	Lucius and Ile goe brave it at the Court,
	I marry will we sir, and weele be waited on.

[Exeunt] ³

Marcus	O heavens!
Buckup	Can you heare a good man grone
speech	And not relent, or not compassion him?
130	Marcus attend him in his extasie,
	That hath more scars of sorrow in his heart,
	Then foe-mens markes upon his batter'd shield,
	But yet so just, that he will not revenge,
	Revenge the heavens for old Andronicus.

[Exit]

**ENTER ARON, CHIRON AND DEMETRIUS AT ONE DORE: AND AT ANOTHER
DORE YOUNG LUCIUS AND ANOTHER, WITH A BUNDLE OF
WEAPONS, AND VERSES WRIT UPON THEM.**
[Most modern texts create a new scene here, Act Four scene 2]

L 44 - e

135	**Chiron**	Demetrius heeres the sonne of Lucius,
	He hath some message to deliver us.
Aaron	I some mad message from his mad Grandfather.
Boy	My Lords, with all the humblenesse I may,
	I greete your honours from Andronicus,
140	⁴ And pray the Romane Gods confound you both.

L 44 - e / R 44 - e : 4. 1. 107 - 4. 2. 6

w₁ Q1/most modern texts = 'base', Q2 - 3/Ff = 'bad'

PCT₂ F1 - 2 set a colon, as if Titus interrupts him: Qq/F3/most modern texts set a period

SD₃ most modern texts indicate all leave, save Marcus

A₄ most modern texts suggest this is spoken as an aside

Demetrius	Gramercie lovely Lucius, what's the newes?
{Boy} [1]	For villainie's [2] markt with rape.

                                             May it please you,
My Grandsire well advis'd hath sent by me,
145   The goodliest weapons of his Armorie,
To gratifie your honourable youth,
The hope of Rome, for so he bad [3] me say :
And so I do and with his gifts present
Your Lordships,[4] when ever you have need,
150   You may be armed and appointed well,
And so I leave you both : like bloody villaines. [5]

[Exit]

Demetrius	What's heere? a scrole, & written round about?
	Let's see.

> *Integer vitae scelerisque purus,* ° *non egit maury iaculis nec ar-*
> 155 *cus .* °[6]

Chiron	O 'tis a verse in Horace, I know it well.
	I read it in the Grammer long agoe.
Aaron as **•Moore•** [7]	I just, a verse in Horace : right, you have it, —[8] Now what a thing it is to be an Asse?

160   Heer's no sound jest, the old man hath found their guilt,
And sends the [9] weapons wrapt about with lines,
That wound (beyond their feeling) to the quick :
But were our witty Empresse well a foot,
She would applaud Andronicus conceit :
165   But let her rest, in her unrest a while.

R 44 - e : 4. 2. 7 - 31

P/ADD [1] F1 omits the prefix set by Qq/F2/most modern texts: also most modern texts start the speech by adding a Qq
line omitted by Ff, 'That you are both discipherd, thats the newes,' indicating the first sentence is an aside

W [2] Qq/F2/most modern texts = 'villaines', F1 = 'villainie's'

W [3] Q1 - 2/most modern texts = 'bid', Q3/Ff = 'bad'

W [4] Qq/Ff set a nine syllable line: both for clarity and to create pentameter most modern texts add 'that'

W [5] most modern texts suggest the last three words are spoken as an aside

VP [6] most modern texts set the Latin as two lines of verse, and from various sources correct the second line to
read 'Non eget Mauri iaculis, nec arcu.'

P [7] as Aaron realises Titus has deciphered Tamora's sons' complicity and is playing games with them, so his
prefix moves from the personal one used by Tamora and her sons ('Aaron') to the much more mask like
persona of 'Moore': Ff maintain this switch until the entrance of the Nurse (see footnote #6, next page), Qq
set 'Moore' for just this one speech, while most modern texts usually maintain the constant prefix 'Aaron'
throughout

A [8] most modern texts indicate this line and the following sentence are spoken as an aside

W [9] Q1 - 2/most modern texts = 'them', Q3/Ff = 'the'

		And now young Lords, was't not[1] a happy starre
		Led us to Rome strangers, and more then so ;
		Captives, to be advanced to this height?
		It did me good before the Pallace gate,
170		To brave the Tribune in his brothers hearing.
	Demetrius	But me more good, to see so great a Lord
		Basely insinuate, and send us gifts.
	Moore	Had he not reason Lord Demetrius?
		Did you not use his daughter very friendly?
175	Demetrius	I would we had a thousand Romane Dames
		At such a bay, by turne to serve our lust.
	Chiron	A charitable wish, and full of love.
	Moore	Heere lack's but you [2] mother for to say, Amen.
	Chiron	And that would she for twenty thousand more.
180	Demetrius	Come, let us go, and pray to all the Gods
		For our beloved mother in her paines.
	Moore	Pray to the devils, the gods have given us over.

FLOURISH

	Demetrius	Why do the Emperors trumpets flourish thus?
	Chiron	Belike for joy the Emperour [3] hath a sonne.
185	Demetrius	Soft, who comes heere?

ENTER NURSE WITH A BLACKE A MOORE CHILDE

	Nurse	Good [4] morrow Lords :
		O tell me, did you see Aaron the Moore? [5]
	•Aaron• [6]	Well, more or lesse, or nere a whit at all,
		Heere Aaron is, and what with Aaron now?

R 44 - c : 4. 2. 32 - 54

W 1 F2/most modern texts = 'was't not', F1 = 'wa's tnot'

W 2 Qq/F3/most modern texts = 'your', F1 - 2 = 'you'

W 3 F2/most modern texts = 'Emperour', F1 = 'Emper our'

W 4 most modern texts follow Q1 - 2 and set 'God', Q3/Ff = 'Good'

LS 5 at least one modern text follows Qq and set the Nurse's opening speech as one fourteen syllable line

P 6 as Aaron begins to deal with the evidence of his adultery that could destroy himself, and all those connected with him (Tamora and her sons), so his personal prefix returns

190	Nurse	Oh gentle Aaron, we are all undone, Now helpe, or woe betide thee evermore.
	Aaron	Why, what a catterwalling dost thou keepe? What dost thou wrap and fumble in *thine armes?
195	Nurse	O that which I would hide from heavens eye, Our Empresse shame, and stately[†1] Romes disgrace, She is delivered Lords, she is delivered.
	Aaron	To whom?
	Nurse	I meane she is brought a bed?[)]
200	Aaron	Wel God give her good rest,[2] What hath he sent her?
	Nurse	A devill.
	Aaron	Why then she is the Devils Dam : a joyfull issue.
205	Nurse	A joylesse, dismall, blacke &, sorrowfull issue, Heere is the babe as loathsome as a toad, Amongst the fairest[3] breeders of our clime, The Empresse sends it thee, thy stampe, thy seale, And bids thee christen it with thy daggers point.
	Aaron	Out you[4] whore, is black so base a hue? Sweet blowse, you are a beautious blossome sure.
210	Demetrius	Villaine what hast thou done?
	Aaron	That which thou canst not undoe.
	Chiron	Thou hast undone our mother. ∞[5]
215	Demetrius	And therein hellish dog, thou hast undone, Woe to her chance, and damn'd her loathed choyce, Accur'st the off-spring of so foule a fiend.

R 44 - e

R 45 - e / L 45 - e : 4. 2. 55 - 79

[W]1 F3/most modern texts = 'and stately', F1 - 2 = 'andstately'

[PCT]2 Qq/F1 set a comma, as if Aaron quickly speeds on to what concerns him most, the child (especially its appearance): F2 sets a period, which some modern texts enlarge to an exclamation point

[W]3 Q1 - 2 = 'fairefast', Q3/Ff = 'fairest', some modern texts = 'fair-faced'

[O]4 Qq/most modern texts set the oath 'Zounds, ye', which Ff reduce to 'Out, ye' because of the provisions of the Acte to restraine the Abuses of Players, 1606 (which restricted on-stage blasphemy and/or profanity)

[ADD]5 Qq/most modern texts set Aaron's amazingly blunt reply 'Villaine I have done the mother.' omitted by Ff, and add Q1- 2's 'her' to the end of the next line, a word omitted by Q3/Ff

Chiron	It shall not live.
Aaron	It shall not die.
Nurse	Aaron it must, the mother wils it so.
Aaron	What, must it Nurse?
220	Then let no man but I
	Doe execution on my flesh and blood.
Demetrius	Ile broach the Tadpole on my Rapiers point :
	Nurse give it me, my sword shall soone dispatch it.
Aaron	Sooner this sword shall plough thy bowels up. [1]
225	Stay murtherous villaines, will you kill your brother?
	Now by the burning Tapers of the skie,
	That sh'one [2] so brightly when this Boy was got,
	He dies upon my Semitars sharpe point,
	That touches this my first borne sonne and heire.
230	I tell you young-lings, [3] not Enceladus
	With all his threatning band of Typhons broode,
	Nor great Alcides, nor the God of warre,
	Shall ceaze this prey out of his fathers hands :
	What, what, ye sanguine shallow harted Boyes,
235	Ye white-limb'd [4] walls, ye Ale-house painted signes,
	Cole-blacke is better then another hue,
	In that it scornes to beare another hue :
	For all the water in the Ocean,
	Can never turne the Swans blacke legs to white,
240	Although she lave them hourely in the flood :
	Tell the Empresse from me, I am of age
	To keepe mine owne, excuse it how she can.
Demetrius	Wilt thou betray thy noble mistris thus?
Aaron	My mistris is my mistris : this my selfe,
245	The vigour, [5] and the picture of my youth :
	This, before all the world do I preferre,
	This mauger all the world will I keepe safe,
	Or some of you shall smoake for it in Rome.

L 45 - e : 4. 2. 80 - 111

SD [1] some modern texts suggest Aaron seizes the child and/or draws his sword

W [2] Qq/F3/most modern texts = 'shone', F1 - 2 = 'sh'one'

W [3] the single word 'ling', a commonplace fish, was in wide usage at the time of the play: thus as set in F1 - 2 'young-lings' has a fine insulting as well as descriptive ring: Qq/F3/most modern texts = 'younglings'

W [4] Q1/F3/most modern texts = 'whitelinde', Q2 - 3/F1 - 2 = 'white-limb'd'

W [5] most modern texts set Qq/Ff's 'vigour', one gloss = 'figure'

Demetrius	By this our mother is for ever sham'd.
250 **Chiron**	Rome will despise her for this foule escape.
Nurse	The Emperour in his rage will doome her death.
Chiron	I blush to thinke upon this ignominie. [1]
Aaron	Why ther's the priviledge your beauty beares :
	Fie trecherous hue, that will betray with blushing
255	The close enacts and counsels of the [2] hart :
	Heer's a young Lad fram'd of another leere,
	Looke how the blacke slave smiles upon the father ;
	As who should say, old Lad I am thine owne.
	He is your brother lords, sensibly fed
260	Of that selfe blood that first gave life to you,
	And from that [3] wombe where you imprisoned were
	He is infranchised and come to light :
	Nay he is your brother by the surer side,
	Although my seale be stamped in his face.
265 **Nurse**	Aaron what shall I say unto the Empresse?
Demetrius	Advise thee Aaron, what is to be done, L 45 - e
	And we will all subscribe to thy advise :
	Save thou the child, so we may all be safe.
Aaron	Then sit we downe and let us all consult.
270	My sonne and I will have the winde of you :
	Keepe there,[4] now talke at pleasure of your safety.
Demetrius	[5] How many women saw this childe of his?
Aaron	Why so brave Lords, when we [6] joyne in league
	I am a Lambe : but if you brave the Moore,
275	The chafed Bore, the mountaine Lyonesse,
	The Ocean swells not so at [7] Aaron stormes :
	But say againe, how many saw the childe?

L 45 - e / R 45 - e : 4. 2. 112 - 140

[1] Qq/most modern texts = 'ignomy', Ff = 'ignominie'

[2] Q1 - 2/most modern texts = 'thy', Q3/Ff = 'the'

[3] Q1 - 2/some modern texts = 'your', Q3/Ff/some modern commentators = 'that'

SD [4] some modern texts suggest they all, or some of them, sit: others leave Aaron standing, supposedly an easier position for killing the Nurse (though murdering her while seated could be an equally terrifying moment)

WHO [5] most modern texts suggest this is spoken to the Nurse

[6] Qq/F1 set a nine syllable line, allowing a moment's (suspicious? amused?) hesitation for Aaron: to establish pentameter, F2 sets 'we all joyne', while modern glosses include 'we do join' and 'we are join'd'

[7] Qq/most modern texts = 'as', Ff = 'at'

Nurse	Cornelia, the midwife, and my selfe,
	And none ¹ else but the delivered Empresse.
280 Aaron	The Empresse, the Midwife, and your selfe,
	Two may keepe counsell, when the the ² third's away :
	Goe to the Empresse, tell her this I said,

[He kils her]

Weeke, weeke, so cries a Pigge prepared to th'spit.

Demetrius	What mean'st thou Aaron? → ³
285	Wherefore did'st thou this?
Aaron	O Lord sir, 'tis a deed of pollicie?

Shall she live to betray this guilt of our's :
A long tongu'd babling Gossip?
                                        No Lords no :
290 And now be it knowne to you my full intent.

Not farre, one Muliteus my Country-man
His wife but yesternight was brought to bed,
His childe is like to her, faire as you are :
Goe packe with him, and give the mother gold,
295 And tell them both the circumstance of all,
And how by this their Childe shall be advaunc'd,
And be received for the Emperours heyre,
And substituted in the place of mine,
To calme this tempest whirling in the Court,
300 And let the Emperour dandle him for his owne.

Harke ye Lords, *ye see I have given her physicke
And you must needs bestow her funerall,
The fields are neere, and you are gallant Groomes :
This done, see that you take no longer daies
305 But send the Midwife presently to me.

The Midwife and the Nurse well made away,
Then let the Ladies tattle what they please.

Chiron	Aaron I see thou wilt not trust the ayre° with secrets. †
Demetrius	For this care of Tamora,° ⁴

ᵂ ₁ Qq/most modern texts = 'no-one', Ff = 'none'

ᵂ ₂ F1 sets an extra 'the', not set by Qq/F2 - 4/most modern texts

ˢᴾ/ˢᴰ ₃ this pair of Ff only short lines (5/5 syllables) sets up a silent (amazed?) moment before Demetrius
continues: most modern texts follow Q and set the two lines as one: also the texts which suggested earlier
Chiron and Demetrius sat, now suggest they rise

ᴸˢ ₄ Qq/Ff set two irregular lines (13/7 syllables) suggesting an outburst from Chiron, and a (careful?) delay before
Demetrius speaks: most modern texts readjust the passage to two normal lines as shown

310   Her selfe, and hers are highly bound to thee.

                             [Exeunt] [1]

Aaron   Now to the Gothes as swift as Swallow flies,
                 There to dispose this treasure in mine armes,
                 And secretly to greete the Empresse friends?
                 Come on you thick-lipt-slave, Ile beare you hence,

315   For it is you that puts us to our shifts:
                 Ile make you feed [2] on berries, and on rootes,
                 And feed on curds and whay, and sucke the Goate,
                 And cabbin in a Cave, and bring you up
                 To be a warriour, and command a Campe.

                             [Exit]
ENTER TITUS, OLD MARCUS, YOUNG LUCIUS, AND OTHER [t3] GENTLEMEN
WITH BOWES, AND TITUS BEARES THE ARROWES WITH
LETTERS ON THE END OF THEM
[Most modern texts create a new scene here, Act Four scene 2]

320   **Titus**   Come Marcus, come, kinsmen this is the way.
                 Sir Boy let me see your Archerie,
                 Looke yee draw home enough, and 'tis there straight:
                 Terras Astrea reliquit,° be you remembred Marcus.
                 She's gone, she's fled,° sirs take you to your tooles,

325   You Cosens° shall goe sound the Ocean:
                 And cast your nets,° haply you may find [4] her in the Sea,° [5]
                 Yet ther's as little justice as at Land:
                 No Publius and Sempronius, you must doe it,   R 45 - e
                 'Tis you must dig with Mattocke, and with Spade,

330   And pierce the inmost Center of the earth:
                 Then when you come to Plutoes Region,
                 I pray you deliver him this petition,
                 Tell him it is for justice, and for aide,
                 And that it comes from old Andronicus,

335   Shaken with sorrowes in ungratefull Rome.
                 Ah Rome!
                        Well, well, I made thee miserable,
                 What time I threw the peoples suffrages
                 On him that thus doth tyrannize ore me.

R 45 - e / L 46 - e   : 4. 3. 171 - 4. 3. 20

SD 1   most modern texts add that Chiron and Demetrius take the body of the Nurse with them

W 2   Qq/Ff/most modern texts = 'feed': modern glosses include 'fat' and 'feat'

SD/N 3   Qq/F2-4 = 'and other', F1 sets a blur which could be either 'andat her' or 'andot her': most modern texts set
    'other', but include the names of those referred to during the scene, viz. Publius, Sempronius and Caius

W 4   Q1 - 2/most modern texts = 'catch', Q3/Ff = 'find'

LS 5   Qq/Ff set four irregular lines (15/10/9 or 10/13 syllables) suggesting Titus' excitement: most modern texts
    set five lines as shown (8/11/9/10 or 11/10 with 'happily' being set for Ff's 'haply'), reducing his intensity

340
Goe get you gone, and pray be carefull all,
And leave you not a man of warre unsearcht,
This wicked Emperour may have shipt her hence,
And kinsmen then we may goe pipe for justice.

Marcus
O Publius is not this a heavie case
345
To see thy Noble Unckle thus distract?

Publius
Therefore my Lords [1] it highly us concernes,
By day and night t'attend him carefully:
And feede his humour kindely as we may,
Till time beget some carefull remedie.

350 **Marcus**
Kinsmen, his sorrowes are past remedie. [2]

Joyne with the Gothes, and with revengefull warre,
Take wreake on Rome for this ingratitude,
And vengeance on the Traytor Saturnine.

Titus
Publius how now? how now my Maisters?
355
What have you met with her?

Publius
No my good Lord, but Pluto sends you word,
If you will have revenge from hell you shall,
Marrie for justice she is so [3] imploy'd,
He thinkes with Jove in heaven, or some where else:
360
So that perforce you must needs stay a time.

Titus
He doth me wrong to feed me with delayes,
Ile dive into the burning Lake below,
And pull her out of Acdron [4] by the heeles.

Marcus we are but shrubs, no Cedars we
365
No big-bon'd-men, fram'd of the Cyclops size,
But mettall Marcus, steele to the very backe,
Yet wrung with wrongs more then our backe [5] can beare:

L 46 · e : 4. 3. 21 - 49

▼ 1 Qq/F1/most modern texts = 'Lords', F2 = 'Lord', as if Publius were addressing only Marcus
F/LS 2 this marks the end of a Q1 page: Q1's catch-word (the word indicating the corresponding word supposedly starting the first line on the next page) is 'But', which does not match what in fact starts the next page, 'If': most commentators suggest that the jump in Marcus' speech (directly from Titus to rebellion) is so abrupt that there must be a line or series of lines missing, (one commentator offers 'But let us live in hope that Lucius will'): thus some modern texts set a single line, empty save for the starting word 'But' to show where this gap may be: however, given the stress Marcus is undergoing, the original 'abruptness' set by Qq/Ff is perfectly understandable, both in terms of character and action
▼ 3 Qq/Ff/most modern texts = 'so', one modern gloss = 'now'
N 4 F2/most modern texts = 'Acheron', Q1 = 'Acaron', while F1's somewhat blurred setting could either be Q1's or the peculiar 'Acdron'
▼ 5 Qq/F2/most modern texts = 'backs', F1 = 'backe'

66

370

And sith there's no justice in earth nor hell,
We will sollicite heaven, and move the Gods
To send downe Justice for to wreake our wongs :
Come to this geare, you are a good Archer Marcus.

HE GIVES THEM THE ARROWES

375

Ad Jovem , that's for you : here *ad Appollonem* ,[1]
Ad Martem, that's for my selfe,
Heere Boy to Pallas, heere to Mercury,
To Saturnine, to Caius, not to Saturnine,[2]
You were as good to shoote against the winde.

Too it Boy, Marcus loose when I bid :
Of my word, I have written to effect,
Ther's not a God left unsollicited.

380

Marcus

Kinsmen, shoot all your shafts into the Court,
We will afflict the Emperour in his pride.

Titus

Now Maisters draw, Oh well said Lucius :
Good Boy in Virgoes lap, give it Pallas.

Marcus

385

My Lord, I aime [3] a Mile beyond the Moone,
Your letter is with Jupiter [4] by this.

Titus

Ha, ha, Publius, Publius, what hast thou done?

See, see, thou hast shot off one of Taurus hornes.

Marcus

390

This was the sport my Lord, when Publius shot,
The Bull being gal'd, gave Aries such a knocke,
That downe fell both the Rams hornes in the Court,
And who should finde them but the Empresse villaine :
She laught, and told the Moore he should not choose
But give them to his Maister for a present.

Titus

Why there it goes, God give your [5] Lordship joy.

L 46 - e

L 46 - e : 4. 3. 50 - 77

N [1] Qq/Ff = 'Appollonem', which most modern texts correct to 'Appollinem'

▼ [2] Qq/Ff set the confusing 'to Saturnine, to Caius, not to Saturnine': most modern texts emend this to 'to Saturne, Caius, not to Saturnine'

▼ [3] Qq/Ff/some modern texts = 'aime', suggesting Marcus is about to let loose his arrow (which he presumably does by the end of the first line, since the second line refers to where it has gone): some modern texts set 'aim'd', suggesting he has shot before he speaks

▼ [4] Q1 sets 'Jubiter' here and three more times: Q2 - 3/Ff change this to 'Jupiter' throughout: most modern texts set 'Jupiter' for the first three readings but set 'Jubiter' for the Clowne (to establish his foolishness?): see footnote #2 next page

▼ [5] Q1 - 2 = 'his', Q3/Ff = 'your'

67

ENTER THE CLOWNE WITH A BASKET AND TWO PIGEONS IN IT

395	Titus	Newes, newes, from heaven, → [1] Marcus the poast is come. Sirrah, what tydings? have you any letters? Shall I have Justice, what sayes Jupiter?
400	Clowne	Ho the Jibbetmaker, he sayes that he hath ta- ken them downe againe, for the man must not be hang'd till the next weeke.
	Titus	But what sayes Jupiter I aske thee?
	Clowne	Alas sir I know not Jupiter: [2] I never dranke with him in all my life. [3]
405	Titus	Why villaine art not thou the Carrier?
	Clowne	I of my Pigions sir, nothing else.
	Titus	Why, did'st thou not come from heaven?

410	Clowne	From heaven?
		  Alas sir, I never came there,
		God forbid I should be so bold, to presse to heaven in my
		young dayes.
		  Why I am going with my pigeons to the
		Tribunall Plebs, to take up a matter of brawle, betwixt
		my Uncle, and one of the Emperialls [4] men.

415	Marcus	Why sir, that is as fit as can be to serve for your Oration, and let him deliver the Pigions to the Emperour from you.
	Titus	Tell mee, can you deliver an Oration to the Em- perour with a Grace?
420	Clowne	Nay truely sir, I could never say grace in all my life. [5]

R 46 - e : 4. 3. 78 - 101

SP [1] the pair of Ff only short lines (4 or 5/6 syllables) allows Titus a moment (of joy?) between the two lines: most modern texts follow Qq and set the two lines as one

W [2] Q1 - 2/most modern texts set 'Jubiter', allowing the Clowne's 'mistakes' to continue: Q3/Ff = 'Jupiter'

VP [3] Qq/Ff set two verse lines (9/10 syllables), allowing the Clowne some (fake?) dignity in his response: most modern texts set his speech in the form he normally speaks, prose: this applies to the first line of his next speech too

W [4] Q1/most modern texts = 'Emperals', Q2 - 3/Ff = 'Emperialls'

OM [5] recent critical commentary suggests dropping this passage, first because Marcus does not speak prose elsewhere in the play, second because the joke is weak: this seems a shame, because the Ff reading shows it is Marcus, the politician, who has the idea of getting to Saturnine through the Clowne: the cut makes it seem Titus' idea

68

Titus	Sirrah come hither, make no more adoe,
	But give your Pigeons to the Emperour,
	By me thou shalt have Justice at his hands.
425	Hold, hold, meane while her's money for thy charges.

> Give me pen and inke.
> Sirrah, can you with a Grace deliver[1] a Supplication?[†2]

Clowne	I sir[3]
Titus	Then here is a Supplication[†4] for you, and when
430	you come to him, at the first approach you must kneele,
	then kisse his foote, then deliver up your Pigeons, and
	then looke for your reward.
	Ile be at hand sir, see you do
	it bravely.
435 **Clowne**	I warrant you sir, let me alone.
Titus	Sirrha hast thou a knife?
	Come let me see it.
	Heere Marcus, fold it in the Oration,
	For thou hast made it like an humble Suppliant:
440	And when thou hast given it[5] the Emperour,
	Knocke at my dore, and tell me what he sayes.
Clowne	God be with you sir, I will.

[Exit]

Titus	Come Marcus let us goe, Publius follow me.

[Exeunt]
ENTER EMPEROUR AND EMPRESSE, AND HER TWO SONNES, THE
EMPEROUR BRINGS THE ARROWES IN HIS HAND
THAT TITUS SHOT AT HIM[6]
[Most modern texts create a new scene here, Act Four Scene 4]

R 46 - e : 4. 3. 102 - 121

[W1] Qq/most modern texts = 'up', Ff omit the word; also F1 = 'Sup plication', F2/most modern texts = 'Supplication'

[LS2] Qq/Ff's two irregular verse lines (5/15 syllables) suggest a momentary outburst from Titus: some modern texts set the passage as continuous prose, somewhat reducing the moment: arguing an incomplete Q1 revision, at least one critic suggests dropping the next eight lines too, though thankfully most commentators agree with Alan Hughes, editor of *The New Cambridge Shakespeare Titus Andronicus*, op. cit., who wryly notes 'perhaps Titus' mind is wandering', page 119, footnote to lines 93 - 112), and maintain the passage

[PCT3] F1 sets no punctuation, as if Titus in his eagerness interrupts him: F2/most modern texts set a period

[W4] F2/most modern texts = 'a Supplication', F1 = 'aSupplication'

[W5] Q1 - 2/most modern texts = 'to', Q3/Ff omit the word

[SD6] in view of the opening line, most modern texts add at the very least 'Attendants' to the entry

˙Saturnine˙[1]	Why Lords, →[2]
445	What wrongs are these? was ever seene
	An Emperour in Rome thus overborne,
	Troubled, Confronted thus, and for the extent
	Of egall[3] justice, us'd in such contempt?
	My Lords, you know the mightfull Gods,[4]
450	(How ever these disturbers of our peace
	Buz in the peoples eares) there nought hath past,
	But even with law against the willfull Sonnes
	Of old Andronicus.
	And what and if
455	His sorrowes have so overwhelm'd his wits,
	Shall we be thus afflicted in his wreakes,
	His fits, his frenzie, and his bitternesse?
	And now he writes to heaven for his redresse.
	See, heeres to Jove, and this to Mercury,
460	This to Appollo, this to the God of warre:
	Sweet scrowles to flie about the streets of Rome:
	What's this but Libelling against the Senate,
	And blazoning our Injustice[5] every where?
	A goodly humour, is it not my Lords?
465	As who would say, in Rome no Justice were.
	But if I live, his fained extasies
	Shall be no shelter to these outrages:
	But he[6] and his shall know, that Justice lives
	In Saturninus health; whom if he[7] sleepe,
470	Hee'l so awake, as he in fury shall
	Cut off the proud'st Conspirator that lives.
Tamora	My gracious Lord, my lovely Saturnine,

R 46 - e

R 46 - e / L 47 - e : 4. 4. 1 - 27

P[1] Saturnine's last appearance was as 'King', but now as the effects of Titus' first public attack manifest themselves, his prefix reverts to the personal 'Saturnine' once again

SP[2] the pair of Ff only short lines (2/8 syllables) allow Saturnine a silent moment to make the most of showing the arrows: most modern texts follow Qq and set the two lines as one

W[3] both F1 ('e gall') and Q1 ('O fegall') lead to most modern texts setting 'egall': F2 sets the more recognisable 'equall'

W[4] Qq/Ff set a somewhat obscure eight syllable line: for clarity and to create pentameter most modern texts emend the line to 'My Lords, you know, as know the mightfull Gods,'

W[5] Qq/most modern texts = 'unjustice', Ff = 'Injustice'

W[6] F2/most modern texts = 'he', F1 = 'h e'

W[7] Qq/Ff/some modern texts set 'he' in both this and the next line : some commentators/modern texts set 'she', since the pronoun refers to 'Justice', traditionally thought in terms of a feminine personification

Lord of my life, Commander of my thoughts,
Calme thee, and beare the faults of Titus age,
475 Th'effects of sorrow for his valiant Sonnes,
Whose losse hath pier'st him deepe, and scar'd his heart;
And rather comfort his distressed plight,
Then prosecute the meanest or the best
For these contempts.
480   Why thus it shall become
High witted Tamora to glose with all:

[Aside] [1]

But Titus, I have touch'd thee to the quicke,
Thy life blood out: If Aaron now be wise,
Then is all safe, the Anchor's [2] in the Port.

ENTER CLOWNE

485   How now good fellow, would'st thou speake with us?

Clowne   Yea forsooth, and your Mistership [3] be Emperiall.

Tamora   Empresse I am, but yonder sits the Emperour.

Clowne   'Tis he; God & Saint Stephen give you good den; [4]
                  I have brought you a Letter, & a couple of Pigions heere.

[He reads the Letter] [5]

490 **Saturnine**   Goe take him away, and hang him presently.

Clowne   How much money must I have?

Tamora   Come sirrah you must be hang'd.

Clowne   Hang'd? ber [6] Lady, then I have brought up a neck
                  to a faire end.

                  [Exit] [7] *Tam lets him go*

L 47 - e : 4. 4. 28 - 49

SD/A [1] this is an exceptionally rare F1 stage direction: most modern texts also consider her previous sentence
an aside

W [2] Q1 - 2/most modern texts = 'Anchor', Q3/Ff = 'Anchor's'

W [3] Q1/most modern texts set the feminine 'Mistriship': Ff set the (mistakenly?) masculine 'Mistership'

O [4] Q1 - 2 set the slightly sacrilegious 'godden', Q3/Ff set the safer 'good den'

SD [5] most modern texts suggest Saturnine is the 'he' who reads the letter

W [6] Qq = 'be', F4 = 'by'r', which most modern texts set as 'by': F1 = 'ber', F2 - 3 = 'bir'

SD [7] Qq/Ff simply set 'exit', leaving the reader to decide whether the Clowne runs away or is escorted out: most
modern texts suggest he is removed as a prisoner

| 495 | Saturnine | Despightfull and intollerable wrongs, |
| | | Shall I endure this monstrous villany? |

I know from whence this same devise proceedes :
May this be borne?
          As if his traytrous Sonnes,
500 That dy'd by law for murther of our Brother,
Have by my meanes beene butcher'd wrongfully?

Goe dragge the villaine hither by the haire,
Nor Age, nor Honour, shall shape priviledge :
For this proud mocke, Ile be thy slaughter man :
505 Sly franticke wretch, that holp'st to make me great,
In hope thy selfe should governe Rome and me.

ENTER NUNTIUS EMILLIUS [1]

Saturnine What newes with thee Emillius?

Emillius Arme my Lords, Rome never had more cause,
The Gothes have gather'd head, and with a power
510 Of high resolved men, bent to the spoyle
They hither march amaine, under conduct
Of Lucius, Sonne to old Andronicus :
Who threats in course of this [2] revenge to do
As much as ever Coriolanus did.

Saturnine as
515 **°King°** [3]   Is warlike Lucius Generall of the Gothes?

These tydings nip me, and I hang the head
As flowers with frost, or grasse beat downe with stormes :
I, now begins our sorrowes to approach,
'Tis he the common people love so much,
520 My selfe hath often heard them say,
(When I have walked like a private man)
That Lucius banishment was wrongfully,
And they have wisht that Lucius were their Emperour.

Tamora Why should you feare?
525   Is not our [4] City strong?   L 47 - e

L 47 - e : 4. 4. 50 - 78

[RCT] 1 most modern texts set a comma between the character's title ('Nuntius', viz. A Messenger) and his name, 'Emillius', which some modern texts spell as Æmilius

[W] 2 Qq/Ff/most modern texts = 'this', one gloss = 'his'

[P] 3 though the ensuing dialogue seems to suggest Saturnine is personally afraid, by reverting to the prefix 'King' once more, Qq/Ff offer the intriguing possibility that he is dealing with matters at a more status-worthy level, perhaps analysing the matter politically, and sometimes, rationally: most modern texts do not set the change

[W] 4 Qq/most modern texts = 'your', Ff = 'our'

King	I, but the Cittizens favour Lucius, And will revolt from me, to succour him.
Tamora	King, be thy thoughts Imperious like thy name. Is the†¹ Sunne dim'd, that Gnats do flie in it?

530
The Eagle suffers little Birds to sing,
And is not carefull what they meane thereby,
Knowing that with the shadow of his wings,
He can at pleasure stint their melodie.

Even so mayest thou, the giddy men of Rome,
535
Then cheare thy spirit, for know thou Emperour,
I will enchaunt the old Andronicus,
With words more sweet, and yet more dangerous
Then baites to fish, or hony stalkes to sheepe,
When as the one is wounded with the baite,
540
The other rotted with delicious foode. ²

King   But he will not entreat†³ his Sonne for us.

Tamora   If Tamora entreat him, then he will,
For I can smooth and fill his aged eare,⁴
With golden promises, that were his heart
545
Almost Impregnable, his old eares deafe,
Yet should both eare and heart obey my tongue.

⁵ Goe thou before to our Embassadour,
Say, that the Emperour requests a parly
Of warlike Lucius, and appoint the meeting.

∞⁶

550   **King**   Emillius do this message Honourably,
And if he stand in ⁷ Hostage for his safety,
Bid him demaund what pledge will please him best.

Emillius   Your bidding shall I do effectually.

[Exit]

R 47 - c : 4. 4. 79 - 107

W₁ F2/most modern texts = 'Is the', F1 = 'Isthe'

W₂ this is one of the rare occasions that a reading from Q3, 'feed', is accepted by most modern texts: Q1 - 2 = 'seede', Ff = 'foode'

W₃ F2/most modern texts = 'entreat', F1 = 'cntreat'

W₄ Q1/most modern texts = 'eares', Q2 - 3/Ff = 'eare'

WHO/W₅ most modern texts indicate this is said to Emillius, and set Qq's 'to be our', rather than Ff's 'to our'

ADD₆ most modern texts add a line from Q1 - 2, omitted by Q3/Ff, viz. 'Even at his Fathers house the old Andronicus.'

W₇ Qq/F1 - 3/most modern texts = 'in', F4 = 'on'

Tamora	Now will I to that old Andronicus,
555	And temper him with all the Art I have,
	To plucke proud Lucius from the warlike Gothes.
	And now sweet Emperour be blithe againe,
	And bury all thy feare in my devises.
˙Saturnine˙ [1]	Then goe successantly [2] and plead for [3] him.

[Exit]

R 47 - c : 4. 4. 108 - 133

[1] at the end of the scene, as once more Tamora appears to rescue the situation, so her husband's 'status' prefix of 'King' disappears, replaced by the personal 'Saturnine'

[2] Qq/Ff/some modern texts = 'successantly', one modern gloss sometimes used = 'incessantly'

[3] Qq/most modern texts = 'to', Ff = 'for'

Actus Quintus

FLOURISH . ENTER LUCIUS WITH AN ARMY OF GOTHES,
WITH DRUM AND SOULDIERS

Lucius	Approved warriours, and my faithfull Friends, I have received Letters from great Rome, Which signifies what hate they beare their Emperour, And how desirous of our sight they are.

5   Therefore great Lords, be as your Titles witnesse,
Imperious and impatient of your wrongs,
And wherein Rome hath done you any scathe,
Let him make treble satisfaction.

Goth [1]   Brave slip, sprung from the Great Andronicus,
10   Whose name was once our terrour, now our comfort,
Whose high exploits, and honourable Deeds,
Ingratefull Rome requites with foule contempt :
Behold [2] in us, weele follow where thou lead'st,
Like stinging Bees in hottest Sommers day,
15   Led by their Maister to the flowred fields,
And be aveng'd on cursed Tamora :
                        [3] And as he saith, so say we all with him.

Lucius   I humbly thanke him, and I thanke you all,
But who comes heere, led by a lusty Goth?

ENTER A GOTH LEADING OF AARON WITH HIS CHILD
IN HIS ARMES

20   Goth   Renowned Lucius, from our troups I straid,
To gaze upon a ruinous Monasterie,   R 47 - e
And as I earnestly did fixe mine eye
Upon the wasted building, suddainely
I heard a childe cry underneath a wall :
25   I made unto the noyse, when soone I heard,
The crying babe control'd with this discourse :
Peace Tawny slave, halfe me, and halfe thy Dam,[4]
Did not thy Hue bewray whose brat thou art?

[P]1 since another Goth shortly enters with Aaron, most modern texts add '1st' to this character's prefix, and '2nd'
to the newly entered character (line 20)

[W]2 Qq/most modern texts = 'Be bold', Ff = 'Behold'

[P]3 most modern texts follow F2 and set this line as a separate speech for 'Omnes', often set as 'All Other Goths'

[W]4 Qq/some modern texts = 'Dame', Q2 - 3/Ff/other modern texts = 'Dam'

30		Had nature lent thee, but thy Mothers looke,
		Villaine thou might'st have bene an Emperour.

Had nature lent thee, but thy Mothers looke,
Villaine thou might'st have bene an Emperour.
But where the Bull and Cow are both milk-white,
They never do beget a cole-blacke-Calfe:
Peace, villaine peace, even thus he rates the babe,
For I must beare thee to a trusty Goth,
Who when he knowes thou art the Empresse babe,
Will hold thee dearely for thy Mothers sake.

With this, my weapon drawne I rusht upon him,
Surpriz'd him suddainely, and brought him hither
To use, as you thinke neeedefull of the man.

Lucius Oh worthy Goth, this is the incarnate devill,
That rob'd Andronicus of his good hand:
This is the Pearle that pleas'd your Empresse eye,
And heere's the Base Fruit of his [1] burning lust.

Say wall-ey'd slave, whether would'st thou convay
This growing Image of thy fiend-like face?

Why dost not speake? what deafe?
[2] Not a word?

A halter Souldiers, hang him on this Tree,
And by his side his Fruite of Bastardie.

Aaron Touch not the boy, he is of Royall blood.

Lucius Too like the Syre for ever being good.
First hang the Child that he may see it sprall,
A sight to vexe the Fathers soule withall.

Aaron [3] Get me a Ladder Lucius, save the Childe,
And beare it from me to the Empresse:
If thou do this, Ile shew thee wondrous things,
That highly may advantage thee to heare;
If thou wilt not, befall what may befall,
Ile speake no more: but [4] vengeance rot you all.

Lucius Say on, and if it please me which thou speak'st,
Thy child shall live, and I will see it Nourisht.

[1] Q1 - 2/most modern texts = her', Q3/Ff = 'his'

[2] Qq/Ff/most modern texts set a nine syllable line, allowing a moment for Aaron's non-reply to register: one metrically minded text destroys this by adding 'What'

[3] Qq/Ff assign the opening phrase to Aaron, suggesting the utmost defiance on his part: most modern texts reassign the command to Lucius: also, most modern texts add a series of directions suggesting some or all of the following; that a ladder is brought, that the baby is removed from Aaron's arms, that Aaron is forced to climb the ladder, that a rope is put about his neck

[4] most modern texts place the last four words in quotation marks

Aaron	And if it please thee? why assure thee Lucius,
	'Twill vexe thy soule to heare what I shall speake :
	For I must talke of Murthers, Rapes, and Massacres,
65	Acts of Blacke-night, abhominable Deeds,
	Complots of Mischiefe, Treason, Villanies
	Ruthfull to heare, yet pittiously preform'd,[1]
	And this shall all be buried by [2] my death,
	Unlesse thou sweare to me my Childe shall live.
70 Lucius	Tell on thy minde, →[3]
	I say thy Childe shall live.
Aaron	Sweare that he shall, and then I will begin.
Lucius	Who should I sweare by, →[4]
	Thou beleevest no God,
75	That graunted, how can'st thou beleeve an oath?
Aaron	What if I do not, as indeed I do not,
	Yet for I know thou art Religious,
	And hast a thing within thee, called Conscience,
	With twenty Popish trickes and Ceremonies,
80	Which I have seene thee carefull to observe :
	Therefore I urge thy oath, for that I know
	An Ideot holds his Bauble for a God,
	And keepes the oath which by that God he sweares,
	To that Ile urge him : therefore thou shalt vow
85	By that same God, what God so ere it be
	That thou adorest, and hast in reverence,
	To save my Boy, to nourish and bring him up,
	Or else I will discover nought to thee.
Lucius	Even by my God I sweare to to [5] thee I will.
90 Aaron	First know thou, →[6]
	I be got him on the Empresse.
Lucius	Oh most Insatiate [7] luxurious woman!

L 48 - e

L 48 - e / R 48 - e : 5. 1. 61 - 88

W [1] F2/most modern texts = 'perform'd', F1 = 'preform'd'

W [2] Q1 - 2/most modern texts = 'in', Q3/Ff = 'by'

SP [3] the Ff only pair of short lines (4/6 syllables) allows for Aaron's refusal to reply before Lucius agrees to save the child's life: most modern texts follow Qq and set the two lines as one

SP [4] the Ff only pair of short lines (5/6 syllables), allowing Lucius a minute hesitation, could well be explained by his perplexity as well as disgust: most modern texts follow Qq and set the two lines as one

W [5] F1 sets the word 'to' twice: Qq/F2 - 4/most modern texts do not set the repetition

SP [6] the Ff only pair of short lines (3/8 syllables) allows Aaron a pause before announceing the mother's identity: most modern texts follow Qq and set the two lines as one: also, F1 = 'be got', F2/most modern texts = 'begot'

W [7] Qq/most modern texts = 'and', Q3/Ff omit the word

Aaron	Tut Lucius, this was but a deed of Charitie,
	To that which thou shalt heare of me anon,
95		'Twas her two Sonnes that murdered Bassianus,
	They cut thy Sisters tongue, and ravisht her,
	And cut her hands off,[1] and trim'd[†2] her as thou saw'st.
Lucius	Oh detestable villaine! → [3]
	Call'st thou that Trimming?
100	Aaron	Why she was washt, and cut, and trim'd,
	And 'twas trim sport for them that had the doing of it.
Lucius	Oh barbarous beastly villaines like thy selfe!
Aaron	Indeede, I was their Tutor to instruct them.
	That Codding spirit had they from their Mother,
105		As sure a Card as ever wonne the Set:
	That bloody minde I thinke they learn'd of me,
	As true a Dog as ever fought at head.
	Well, let my Deeds be witnesse of my worth:
	I trayn'd thy Bretheren to that guilefull Hole,
110		Where the dead Corps of Bassianus lay:
	I wrote the Letter, that thy Father found,
	And hid the Gold within the [4] Letter mention'd.
	Confederate with the Queene, and her two Sonnes,
	And what not done, that thou hast cause to rue,
115		Wherein I had no stroke of Mischeife in it.
	I play'd the Cheater for thy Fathers hand,
	And when I had it, drew my selfe apart,
	And almost[†5] broke my heart with extreame laughter.
	I pried me through the Crevice of a Wall,
120		When for his hand, he had his two Sonnes heads,
	Beheld his teares, and laught so hartily,
	That both mine eyes were rainie like to his:
	And when I told the Empresse of this sport,
	She sounded almost at my pleasing tale,
125 | | And for my tydings, gave me twenty kisses. |

[W1] Qq/most modern texts = 'hands and', Ff = 'hands off, and'

[W2] F2/most modern texts = 'trim'd', F1 = 'crim'd'

[SP3] the Ff only pair of short lines (7/5 syllables) allows a silent moment when Lucius, hearing the callous description of what happened to his sister, forces himself into self-control, or is perhaps restrained by others around him: most modern texts follow Qq and set the two lines as one

[W4] Q1/most modern texts = 'that', Q2 - 3/Ff = 'the'

[W5] F2/most modern texts = 'And almost', F1 = 'Andalmost'

Goth [1]		What canst thou say all this, and never blush?
Aaron		I, like a blacke Dogge, as the saying is.
Lucius		Art thou not sorry for these hainous deedes?

           Aaron

130

135

140

145

I, that I had not done a thousand more :
Even now I curse the day, and yet I thinke
Few come within few [2] compasse of my curse,
Wherein I did not some Notorious ill,
As kill a man, or else devise his death,
Ravish a Maid, or plot the way to do it,
Accuse some Innocent, and forsweare my selfe,
Set deadly Enmity betweene two Friends,
Make poore mens Cattell breake [3] their neckes,
Set fire on Barnes and Haystackes in the night,
And bid the Owners quench them with the [4] teares :
Oft have I dig'd up dead men from their graves,
And set them upright at their deere Friends doore,
Even when their sorrowes almost was forgot,
And on their skinnes, as on the Barke of Trees,
Have with my knife carved in Romaine Letters,
Let not your sorrow die, though I am dead.

Tut, I have done a thousand dreadfull things
As willingly, as one would kill a Fly,
And nothing greeves me hartily indeede,
But that I cannot doe ten thousand more.

150   **Lucius**

Bring downe the divell, for he must not die
So sweet a death as hanging presently. [5]

           Aaron

155

If there be divels, would I were a devill,
To live and burne in everlasting fire,
So I might have your company in hell,   R 48 - e
But to torment you with my bitter tongue.

           Lucius

Sirs stop his mouth, & let him speake no more. [6]

P [1] some texts suggest that the 1st Goth take all the remaining 'Goth' speeches in the scene: Qq/Ff offer no indication as to which of the Goths speaks when

W [2] F1 sets a repetition of the first word of the line 'few': F2/Qq/most modern texts = 'the'

W [3] since Qq/Ff set an eight syllable line, metrically minded commentators have suggested 'silly Cattle', or 'fall and break'

W [4] Qq/most modern texts = 'their', Ff = 'the'

SD [5] most modern texts suggest Aaron is brought down off the ladder

SD [6] most modern texts suggest Aaron is now gagged

ENTER EMILLIUS

Goth	My Lord, there is a Messenger from Rome
	Desires to be admitted to your presence.

Lucius	Let him come neere.

160   Welcome Emillius, what [1] the newes from Rome?

Emillius   Lord Lucius and you Prince of the Gothes,
                The Romaine Emperour greetes you all by me,
                And for he understands you are in Armes,
                He craves a parly at your Fathers house
165   Willing you to demand your Hostages,
                And they shall be immediately delivered.

Goth   What saies our Generall?

Lucius   Emillius, let the Emperour give his pledges
                Unto my Father, and my Uncle Marcus,

[Flourish]

170   And we will come : march away. [2]

[Exeunt]
ENTER TAMORA, AND HER TWO SONNES DISGUISED
[Most modern texts create a new scene here, Act Five Scene 2]

Tamora   Thus in this strange and sad Habilliament,
                I will encounter with Andronicus,
                And say, I am Revenge sent from below,
                To joyne with him and right his hainous wrongs :
175   Knocke at his study where they say he keepes,
                To ruminate strange plots of dire Revenge,
                Tell him Revenge is come to joyne with him,
                And worke confusion on his Enemies.

THEY KNOCKE AND TITUS OPENS HIS STUDY DORE [3]

Titus   Who doth mollest my Contemplation?
180   Is it your tricke to make me ope the dore,
                That so my sad decrees may flie away,
                And all my studie be to no effect?

                You are deceiv'd, for what I meane to do,
                See heere in bloody lines I have set downe :
185   And what is written shall be executed.

L 49 - e   :   5. 1. 152 - 5. 2. 15

[1] Qq/F2/most modern texts = 'whats', F1 = 'what'
SD/ALT/W [2] Qq/Ff set the last two words as dialogue: some modern texts set them as part of a stage direction
SD [3] most modern texts suggest he is 'aloft' and Tamora and her sons have entered 'below'

Tamora		Titus, I am come to talke with thee,[1]
	Titus	No not a word : how can I grace my talke, Wanting a hand to give it action,[2] Thou hast the ods of me, therefore no more.
190	**Tamora**	If thou did'st know me, →[3] Thou would'st talke with me.
	Titus	I am not mad, I know thee well enough, Witnesse this wretched stump, → Witnesse these crimson lines,
195		Witnesse these Trenches made by griefe and care, Witnesse the tyring day, and heavie†[4] night, Witnesse all sorrow, that I know thee well For our proud Empresse, Mighty Tamora : Is not thy comming for my other hand?
200	**Tamora**	Know thou sad man, I am not Tamora, She is thy Enemie, and I thy Friend, I am Revenge sent from th'infernall Kingdome, To ease the gnawing Vulture of the[5] mind, By working wreakefull vengeance on my[6] Foes :
205		Come downe and welcome me to this worlds light, Conferre with me of Murder and of Death, Ther's not a hollow Cave or lurking place, No Vast obscurity, or Misty vale, Where bloody Murther or detested Rape,
210		Can couch for feare, but I will finde them out, And in their eares tell them my dreadfull name, Revenge, which makes the foule offenders[7] quake.
	Titus	Art thou Revenge? and art thou sent to me, To be a torment to mine Enemies?
215	**Tamora**	I am, therefore come downe and welcome me. L 49 - e

[PCT 1] F1 sets no punctuation as if Titus interrupts her, Qq/F2/most modern texts set a period

[W 2] Ff/some modern texts = 'give it action': Qq = 'give that accord', which some modern texts/commentators modify to either 'give 't'that accord', or, 'give it that accord'

[SP 3] as the cat and mouse game develops between Tamora and Titus, Ff alone set two pairs of short lines (5/5 and 6/6 syllables) separated by one normal line: the minute hesitations thus offered allow for the teasing out of the debate: most modern texts follow Qq and set each pair of short lines as one longer line

[W 4] F2/most modern texts = 'and heavie', F1 = 'andheavie'

[W 5] Qq/most modern texts = 'thy', Ff = 'the'

[W 6] Qq/most modern texts = 'thy', Ff = 'my'

[W 7] Q1 - 2/most modern texts = 'offender', Q3/Ff = 'offenders'

Titus	Doe me some service ere I come to thee:
	Loe by thy[t1] side where Rape and Murder stands,
	Now give some surance that thou art Revenge,
	Stab them, or teare them on thy Chariot wheeles,
220	And then Ile come and be thy Waggoner,
	And whirle along with thee about the Globes. [2]
	Provide thee two proper Palfries, as [3] blacke as Jet,
	To hale thy vengefull Waggon swift away,
	And finde out Murder [4] in their guilty cares. [5]
225	And when thy Car is loaden with their heads,
	I will dismount, and by the [6] Waggon wheele,
	Trot like a Servile footeman all day long,
	Even from Eptons [7] rising in the East,
	Untill his very [8] downefall in the Sea.
230	And day by day Ile do this heavy taske,
	So thou destroy Rapine and Murder there.
Tamora	These are my Ministers, and come with me.
Titus	Are them [9] thy Ministers, what are they call'd?
Tamora	Rape and Murder, therefore called so,
235	Cause they take vengeance of such kind of men.
Titus	Good Lord how like the Empresse Sons they are,
	And you the Empresse: But we worldly men,
	Have miserable mad mistaking eyes:
	Oh sweet Revenge, now do I come to thee,
240	And if one armes imbracement will content thee,
	I will imbrace thee in it by and by. [10]

R 49 - e : 5. 2. 44 - 69

[W1] F2/most modern texts = 'by thy', F1 = 'bythy'

[PCT/W2] Qq/Ff/some modern texts = 'Globes', other modern texts = ' globe': also, Qq/Ff set a period, as if the following sentence is an extra enticement that Titus feels he must offer (perhaps because what he has promised so far seems to be having little or no discernible effect on the disguised trio?): most modern texts set a comma

[W3] Q1 - 2/most modern texts omit 'as', thus setting an eleven syllable line, while metrically minded commentators have also suggested dropping 'two' to set pentameter

[W4] Qq/Ff = 'Murder', most modern texts = 'murderers'

[W5] F2/most modern texts = 'caves', Qq/F1 = 'cares'

[W6] Q1 = 'thy', Q2 - 3/Ff = 'the'

[N7] F2/most modern texts set the mythologically correct 'Hyperion': Qq = 'Epeons', F1 = 'Eptons'

[W8] Qq/Ff = 'very', one modern gloss = 'weary'

[W9] F2/most modern texts = 'they', Qq/F1 = 'them'

[SD D] most modern texts suggest Titus exits (above), and enters (below) at the end of Tamora's speech

Tamora		This closing with him, fits his Lunacie,
		What ere I forge to feede his braine-sicke fits,
		Do you uphold, and maintaine in your speeches,
245		For now he firmely takes me for Revenge,
		And being Credulous in this mad thought,
		Ile make him send for Lucius his Sonne,
		And whil'st I at a Banquet hold him sure,
		Ile find some cunning practise out of hand
250		To scatter and disperse the giddie Gothes,
		Or at the least make them his Enemies :
		See heere he comes, and I must play[1] my theame.
Titus		Long have I bene forlorne, and all for thee,
		Welcome dread Fury to my woefull house,
255		Rapine and Murther, you are welcome too,
		How like the Empresse and her Sonnes you are.
		Well are you fitted, had you but a Moore,
		Could not all hell afford you such a devill?
		For well I wote the Empresse never wags ;
260		But in her company there is a Moore,
		And would you represent our Queene aright
		It were convenient you had such a devill :
		But welcome as you are,[2] what shall we doe?
Tamora		What would'st thou have us doe Andronicus?
265 **Demetrius**		Shew me a Murtherer, Ile deale with him.
Chiron		Shew me a Villaine that hath done a Rape,
		And I am sent to be reveng'd on him.
Tamora		Shew me a thousand that have[3] done thee wrong,
		And Ile[4] be revenged on them all.
270 **Titus**		Looke round about the wicked streets of Rome,
		And when thou find'st a man that's like thy selfe,
		Good Murder stab him, hee's a Murtherer.
		Goe thou with him, and when it is thy hap
		To finde another that is like to thee,
275		Good Rapine stab him, he is a Ravisher.

W [1] Qq/most modern texts = 'ply', Ff = 'play'

RCT [2] Qq/Ff and some modern texts set a comma, suggesting a rather (unstable?) slippage from one thought to the next: other modern texts rationalise the moment by setting a period

W [3] Q1/most modern texts = 'hath', Q2 - 3/Ff = 'have'

W [4] Q1/most modern texts = 'I will', Ff = 'Ile'

Go thou with them, and in the Emperours Court,
There is a Queene attended by a Moore,
Well maist ¹ thou know her by *thy owne proportion,
For up and downe she doth resemble thee.

280   I pray thee doe on them some violent death,
They have bene violent to me and mine.   R 49 - e

Tamora   Well hast thou lesson'd us, this shall we do.

But would it please thee good Andronicus,
To send for Lucius thy thrice Valiant Sonne,
285   Who leades towards Rome a Band of Warlike Gothes,
And bid him come and Banquet at thy house.

When he is heere, even at thy Solemne Feast,
I will bring in the Empresse, and her Sonnes,
The Emperour himselfe, and all thy Foes,
290   And at thy mercy shall they stoop, and kneele,
And on them shalt thou ease, thy angry heart :
What saies Andronicus to this devise?

ENTER MARCUS ²

Titus   Marcus my Brother, 'tis sad Titus calls,
Go gentle Marcus to thy Nephew Lucius,
295   Thou shalt enquire him out among the Gothes,
Bid him repaire to me, and bring with him
Some of the chiefest Princes of the Gothes,
Bid him encampe his Souldiers where they are,
Tell him the Emperour, and the Empresse too,
300   Feasts ³ at my house, and he shall Feast with them,
This do thou for my love, and so let him,
As he regards his aged Fathers life.

Marcus   This will I do, and soone returne againe. ⁴

Tamora   Now will I hence about thy businesse,
305   And take my Ministers along with me.

Titus   Nay, nay, let Rape and Murder stay with me,
Or els Ile call my Brother backe againe,
And cleave to no revenge but Lucius.

R 49 - e / L 50 - e : 5. 2. 104 - 136

ᵂ ₁ Q1/most modern texts = 'shalt', Q2 - 3/Ff = 'maist'
ˢᴰ ₂ most modern texts delay the entry until after Titus' next line
ᵂ ₃ Qq/most modern texts = 'Feast', Ff = 'Feasts'
ˢᴰ ₄ most modern texts set an exit for Marcus

Tamora	[1] What say you Boyes, will you bide [2] with him,
310	Whiles I goe tell my Lord the Emperour,
	How I have govern'd our determined jest?
	Yeeld to his Humour, smooth and speake him faire,
	And tarry with him till I turne againe.
Titus	I know them all, though they suppose me mad,[3]
315	And will ore reach them in their owne devises,
	A payre of cursed hell-hounds and their Dam. [4]
Demetrius	Madam depart at pleasure, leave us heere.
Tamora	Farewell Andronicus, revenge now goes
	To lay a complot to betray thy Foes.
320 Titus	I know thou doo'st, and sweet revenge farewell. [5]
Chiron	Tell us old man, how shall we be imploy'd?
Titus	Tut, I have worke enough for you to doe,
	Publius come hither, Caius and Valentine. [6]
Publius	What is your will?
325 Titus	Know you these two?
Publius	The Empresse Sonnes → [7]
	I take them, Chiron, Demetrius.
Titus	Fie Publius, fie, thou art too much deceav'd,
	The one is Murder,[8] Rape is the others name,
330	And therefore bind them gentle Publius,
	Caius, and Valentine, lay hands on them,
	Oft have you heard me wish for such an houre,
	And now I find it, therefore binde them sure,[9]
	∞ [10]

A 1
most modern texts suggest the next three speeches are asides

W 2
Q1/most modern texts set 'abide', creating a ten syllable line: Q2 - 3/Ff = 'bide'

W 3
Q1/most modern texts set the past tense of the verbs, 'knew' and 'supposed': Q2 - 3/Ff set the present tense, 'know' and 'suppose'

W 4
Q3/Ff/most modern texts = 'Dam', Q1 - 2 = 'Dame'

SD 5
most modern texts suggest Tamora now exits

SD 6
most modern texts indicate that three men Titus call for now enter

SP 7
the Ff only pair of short lines (4/8 syllables) allows for a wonderful pause as Publius realises who is at their mercy: most modern texts follow Qq and set the two lines as one

W 8
Q1/some modern texts = 'and', Q2 - 3/Ff/most modern texts omit the word

PCT 9
F1 sets a comma as if Chiron interrupts him: F2 sets a period: Qq add an extra line, see the following footnote

ADD D
most modern texts set a Qq line omitted by Ff, viz. 'And stop their mouthes if they begin to crie.', and add an exit for Titus

	Chiron	Villaines forbeare, we are the Empresse Sonnes.
335	Publius	And therefore do we, what we are commanded.

Stop close their mouthes, let them not speake a word,
Is he sure bound, looke that you binde them fast.

[Exeunt]
ENTER TITUS ANDRONICUS WITH A KNIFE, AND LAVINIA
WITH A BASON

Titus   Come, come Lavinia, looke, thy Foes are bound,
Sirs stop their mouthes, let them not speake to me,

340   But let them heare what fearefull words I utter.   L 50 - e

Oh Villaines, Chiron, and Demetrius,
Here stands the spring whom you have stain'd with mud,
This goodly Sommer with your Winter mixt,
You kil'd her husband, and for that vil'd fault,

345   Two of her Brothers were condemn'd to death,
My hand cut off, and made a merry jest,
Both her sweet Hands, her Tongue, and that more deere
Then Hands or tongue, her spotlesse Chastity,
Inhumaine[†1] Traytors, you constrain'd and for'st.

350   What would you say, if I should let you speake?

Villaines for shame you could not beg for grace.

Harke Wretches, how I meane to martyr you,
This one Hand yet is left, to cut your throats,
Whil'st[2] that Lavinia tweene her stumps doth hold:

355   The Bason that receives your guilty blood.

You know your Mother meanes to feast with me,
And calls herselfe Revenge, and thinkes me mad.

Harke Villaines, I will grin'd your bones to dust,
And with your blood and it, Ile make a Paste,

360   And of the Paste a Coffen I will reare,
And make two Pasties of your shamefull Heads,
And bid that strumpet your unhallowed Dam,
Like to the earth swallow her[3] increase.

This is the Feast, that I have bid her to,

365   And this the Banquet she shall surfet on,
For worse then Philomel you us'd[†4] my Daughter,

[w1] F2/most modern texts = 'Inhumaine', F1 = ' Iuhumaine'

[w2] Q1/most modern texts = 'Whiles', Q1 - 2/Ff = 'Whil'st'

[w3] Qq/most modern texts = 'owne', setting a ten syllable line: Ff omit the word

[w4] F2/most modern texts = 'us'd', F1 = 'us d'

And worse then Progne ¹ I will be reveng'd,
And now prepare your throats: Lavinia come.

Receive the blood, and when that they are dead,
370 Let me goe grin'd their Bones to powder small,
And with this hatefull Liquor temper it,
And in that Paste let their vil'd Heads be bakte,
Come, come, be every one officious,
To make this Banket, which I wish might ² prove,
375 More sterne and bloody then the Centaures Feast.

[He cuts their throats]

So now bring them in, for Ile play the Cooke,
And see them ready, gainst ³ their Mother comes.

[Exeunt]
ENTER LUCIUS, MARCUS, AND THE GOTHES ⁴
[Most modern texts create a new scene here, Act Five Scene 3]

Lucius   Unckle Marcus, since 'tis my Fathers minde
That I repair to Rome, I am content.

380 Goth   And ours with thine befall, what Fortune will.

Lucius   Good Unckle take you in this barbarous Moore,
This Ravenous Tiger, this accursed devill,
Let him receive no sustenance, fetter him,
Till he be brought unto the Emperours †⁵ face,
385 For testimony of her foule proceedings.
And see the Ambush of our Friends be strong,
If ere ⁶ the Emperour meanes no good to us.

Aaron   Some devill whisper curses in *my eare,
And prompt me that my tongue may utter forth,†⁷
390 The Venemous Mallice of my swelling heart.

Lucius   Away Inhumaine Dogge, Unhallowed Slave,
Sirs, helpe out Unckle, to convey him in, ⁸

R 50 - e : 5. 2. 195 - 5. 3. 15

ᴺ ₁ most modern texts set the mythologically correct 'Procne', Qq/F4= 'Progne', F1 - 3 = 'Progue'

ᵂ ₂ Qq/most modern texts = 'may', Ff = 'might'

ᵂ ₃ though an eleven syllable line results, most modern texts follow Qq and set 'against': Ff = 'gainst'

ˢᴰ ₄ since both characters are referred to in the scene, modern texts usually add both Aaron, under guard, and his son to the entry

ᵂ ₅ Q1 - 2 = 'Empresse' which most modern texts set as 'empress', Q3 = 'Emperours', Ff = 'Emprous'

ᵂ ₆ Qq/F2 = 'I feare', F1 = 'If ere'

ᵂ ₇ F2/most modern texts = 'forth', F1 = 'for th'

ˢᴰ ₈ most modern texts suggest Aaron is taken out under guard

[Flourish] — people or noise   5. 1. 393 - 416

The Trumpets shew the Emperour is at hand.

SOUND TRUMPETS. ENTER EMPEROUR AND EMPRESSE, WITH TRIBUNES AND OTHERS [1]

Saturnine [2]	What, hath the Firemament [3] more Suns then one?
395 Lucius	What bootes it thee to call thy selfe a Sunne?
Marcus	Romes Emperour & Nephewe breake the parle

Romes Emperour & Nephewe breake the parle
These quarrels must be quietly debated,
The Feast is ready which the carefull Titus,   R 50 - e
Hath ordained to an Honourable end,
For Peace, for Love, for League, and good to Rome :
Please you therefore draw nie and take your places.

Saturnine   Marcus we will.

[Hoboyes]
A TABLE BROUGHT IN .
ENTER TITUS LIKE A COOKE, PLACING THE MEAT ON THE TABLE, AND LAVINIA WITH A VALE OVER HER FACE [4]

Titus   Welcome my [5] gracious Lord, → [6]
Welcome Dread Queene,
Welcome ye Warlike Gothes, welcome Lucius,
And welcome all : although the cheere be poore,
'Twill fill your stomacks, please you eat of it.

Saturnine   Why art thou thus attir'd Andronicus?

Titus   Because I would be sure to have all well,
To entertaine your Highnesse, and your Empresse.

Tamora   We are beholding to you good Andronicus?

Titus   And if your Highnesse knew my heart, you were :
My Lord the Emperour resolve me this,
Was it well done of rath Virginius,
To slay his daughter with his owne right hand,
Because she was enfor'st, stain'd, and deflowr'd?

R 50 - e / L 51 - e : 5. 3. 16 - 38

SD 1   since he is referred to later in the scene, most modern texts add the name of Emillius to the entry

P 2   Ff maintain Saturnine's personal prefix throughout, Qq switch to the formal 'King': most modern texts follow Ff

W 3   Qq/F2/most modern texts = 'Firmament', F1 = 'Firemament'

SD 4   most modern texts add Young Lucius to the entry

W 5   Q2 - 3/Ff/some modern texts = 'gracious', which Q1 and other modern texts omit

SP 6   this pair of Ff only short lines (6/4 syllables) allows time for Titus to make the most of his welcome: most modern texts follow Qq and set the two lines as one

Saturnine	It was Andronicus.
Titus	Your reason, Mighty Lord?[}]
Saturnine	Because the Girle, should not survine her shame,
420	And by her presence still renew his sorrowes.
Titus	A reason mighty, strong, and ¹ effectuall,
	A patterne, president, and lively warrant,
	For me (most wretched) to performe the like : ²
	Die, die, Lavinia, and thy shame with thee,
425	And with thy shame, thy Fathers sorrow die.

[He kils her]

Saturnine	What hast ³ done, unnaturall and unkinde?
Titus	Kil'd her for whom my teares have made me blind.
	I am as wofull as Virginius was,
	And have a thousand times more cause then he.

∞ ⁴

430	**Saturnine**	What was she ravisht? tell who did the deed,⁵
Titus	Wilt please you eat, →⁶
	Wilt please your Highnesse feed?
Tamora	Why hast thou slaine thine onely Daughter?
Titus	Not I, 'twas Chiron and Demetrius,
435	They ravisht her, and cut away her tongue,
	And they, 'twas they, that did her all this wrong.
Saturnine	Go fetch them hither to us presently.
Titus	Why there they are both, baked in that Pie,⁷

^W ₁ Qq/Ff set 'and', which some modern commentators suggest omitting for metrical reasons

^{SD} ₂ at least one modern text adds the (probably unnecessary) direction that Titus now unveils Lavinia, though others suggest he do so after killing her

^W ₃ Qq/most modern texts set 'thou', Ff omit the word

^{ADD} ₄ most modern texts set a Qq line omitted by Ff, viz. 'To doe this outrage, and it now is done.' (with Q3 setting 'is now')

^{PCT} ₅ F1 - 2 set a comma, as if Titus' apparent nonchalant non-sequitur interrupts Saturnine: Qq/F3/most modern texts set a period

^{SP} ₆ this pair of Ff only short lines (4/6 syllables) allows for the silent responses from everyone in the room to be fully registered: most modern texts follow Qq and set the two lines as one

^{SD} ₇ the thrill of adding extra grand guignol stage directions seems very difficult for some modern texts to resist: here, for example, one text suggests Titus reveals the heads of the two sons baked in the pie

		Whereof their Mother dantily ¹ hath fed,	
440		Eating the flesh that she herselfe hath bred.	
		'Tis true, 'tis true, witnesse my knives sharpe point.	
		[He stabs the Empresse]	
	Saturnine ²	Die franticke wretch, for this accursed deed. ³	
	Lucius	Can the Sonnes eye, behold his Father bleed? _ Saṭi Killed	
		There's meede for meede, death for a deadly deed. ⁴	
445	Marcus	You sad fac'd men, people and Sonnes of Rome,	
		By uprores sever'd like ⁵ a flight of Fowle,	
		Scattred by windes and high tempestuous gusts :	
		Oh let me teach you how, to knit againe	
		This scattred Corne, into one mutuall sheafe,	
450		These broken limbs againe into one body.	
	Goth ⁶	Let Rome herselfe be bane unto herselfe,	
		And shee whom mightie kingdomes cursie too,	
		Like a forlorne and desperate castaway,	
		Doe shamefull execution on her selfe. ⁷	
455		But if my frostie signes and chaps of age,	
		Grave witnesses of true experience,	
		Cannot induce you to attend my words,	
		Speake Romes deere friend, as 'erst our Auncestor,	L 51 - e
		When with his solemne tongue he did discourse	
460		To love-sicke Didoes sad attending eare,	
		The story of that balefull burning night,	
		When subtil Greekes †⁸ surpriz'd King Priams Troy :	
		Tell us what Sinon hath bewicht our eares,	
		Or who hath brought the fatall engine in,	
465		That gives our Troy, our Rome the civill wound.	

L 51 - e / R 51 - e : 5. 3. 61 - 87

W ¹ F1 - 3 = 'dantily', Qq/F4/most modern texts = 'daintily'

P ₂ for his last speech, Qq change the prefix from 'King' to 'Emperour': Ff maintain the personal 'Saturnine' used throughout the scene: most modern texts follow Ff

SD ₃ most modern texts indicate Saturnine now kills Titus

SD ₄ most modern texts indicate that Lucius now kills Saturnine: others add that the Goths rush in to protect the Andronicy, who under their protection manage to 'escape aloft': with or without Gothic interference, most modern texts indicate that both Marcus and Lucius now speak from 'aloft'

W ₅ Q1 - 2/most modern texts = 'as', Q3/Ff = 'like'

P/W ₆ Qq assign this speech to a Roman Lord, whom some modern texts assume to be Emillius: two critics suggest the speech should continue as part of Marcus' opening, altering Qq/Ff's 'Let' to 'Least': Ff assign the speech to a Goth, as shown

PCT ₇ though both Qq and Ff set a period here, some modern texts diminish the opening warning by setting a comma, and allowing the speech to directly proceed with a possible saving solution: texts repunctuating Qq/Ff then set in three lines time a period instead of a comma

W ₈ F1 = 'subtilGreekes', F2/most modern texts = 'subtill Greekes'

¹ My heart is not compact of flint nor steele,
Nor can I utter all our bitter griefe,
But floods of teares will drowne my Oratorie,
And breake my very ² uttrance, even in the time
470   When it should move *you to attend me most,
Lending your kind hand ³ Commiseration.

Heere is a ⁴ Captaine, let him tell the tale,
Your hearts will throb ⁵ and weepe to heare him speake.

Lucius   This Noble ⁶ Auditory, be it knowne to you,
475   That cursed Chiron and ⁷ Demetrius
Were they that murdred our Emperours Brother,
And they it were that ravished our Sister,
For their fell faults our Brothers were beheaded,
Our Fathers teares despis'd, and basely cousen'd,
480   Of that true hand that fought Romes quarrell out,
And sent her enemies unto the grave.

Lastly, my selfe unkindly banished,
The gates shut on me, and turn'd weeping out,
To beg reliefe among Romes Enemies,
485   Who drown'd their enmity in my true teares,
And op'd their armes to imbrace me as a Friend:
And I am ⁸ turned forth, be it knowne to you,
That have preserv'd her welfare in my blood,
And from her bosome tooke the Enemies point,
490   Sheathing the steele in my adventrous body.

Alas you know, I am no Vaunter I,
My scars can witnesse, dumbe although they are,
That my report is just and full of truth:
But soft, me thinkes I do digresse too much,
495   Cyting my worthlesse praise: Oh pardon me,
For when no Friends are by, men praise themselves.

P/L ₁   R 51 - e : 5. 3. 88 - 118
though Qq/Ff set this as a continuation of the Roman's speech, at least one text suggests Marcus begins to
speak now: for further details see *The Arden Shakespeare Titus Andronicus*, op. cit., page 270, footnote to line 87
W ₂
Q3/Ff = 'my very', Q1 - 2/most modern texts = 'my'
COMP/W ₃
this and the next four footnotes deal with the effects of the last five lines of a damaged Q1 page:
commentators argue the Q2 compositor using the damaged Q1 text to set copy had to guess at the beginning of
each line: revisions became possible when an undamaged Q1 copy surfaced - an enormous aid to modern
scholarship: here, Q1 /most modern texts = 'And force you', Q2 - 3 = 'Lending your kind', Ff = the very strange
'Lending your kind hand'
W ₄
Q1 = 'Her's Romes young' which most modern texts set, altering 'Her's' to 'Here's': Q2 - 3/Ff = 'Heere is a'
W ₅
Q1/most modern texts = 'Whiles I stand by', Q2 - 3/Ff = 'Your hearts will throb'
W ₆
Q1/most modern texts = 'Then gracious', Q2 - 3 = 'Then, noble', Ff = 'This Noble'
W ₇
Q1/most modern texts = 'That Chiron and the damn'd', Q2 -3/Ff = 'That cursed Chiron and'
W ₈
Q1 - 2/most modern texts = 'I am the', Q3/Ff = 'And I am'

Marcus	Now is my turne to speake: Behold this [1] Child,
	Of this was Tamora delivered,
	The issue of an Irreligious Moore,
500	Chiefe Architect and plotter of these woes,
	The Villaine is alive in Titus house,
	And [2] as he is, to witnesse this is true.

Now judge what course [3] had Titus to revenge
These wrongs, unspeakeable past patience,
505 Or more then any living man could beare.

Now you have [4] heard the truth, what say you Romaines?

Have we done ought amisse? shew us wherein,
And from the place where you behold us now,[5]
The poore remainder of Andronici,
510 Will hand in hand all headlong cast us downe,[6]
And on the ragged stones beat forth our braines,[7]
And make a mutuall closure of our house:
Speake Romaines speake, and if you say we shall,
Loe hand in hand, Lucius and I will fall.

515 Emillius   Come come, thou reverent [8] man of Rome,
And bring our Emperour gently in thy hand,
Lucius our Emperour: for well I know,
The common voyce do cry it shall be so.

Marcus [9]   Lucius, all haile Romes Royall Emperour,
520   [10]   Goe, goe into old Titus sorrowfull house,
And hither hale that misbelieving Moore,
To be adjudg'd some direfull slaughtering death,
As punishment for his most wicked life.
[11] Lucius all haile to Romes gracious Governour.   R 51 - e

---

R 51 - e : 5. 3. 119 - 146

[1] Q1 - 2/most modern texts = 'the', Q3/Ff = 'this'

[2] Qq/Ff = 'And', one modern gloss = 'Damn'd'

[3] F4/most modern texts = 'cause', Qq/F1 - 3 = 'course'

[4] Qq/most modern texts = 'have you', Ff = 'you have'

COMP/V [5] this and the next two footnotes deal with lines at the bottom of the reverse side of the damaged Q1 page referred to in footnote #3, previous page: here, Q1/most modern texts = 'pleading', Q2 - 3/Ff = 'now'

[6] Q1/most modern texts = 'hurle our selves', Q2 - 3/Ff = 'cast us downe'

[7] Q1/most modern texts = 'soules', Q2 - 3/Ff = 'braines'

[8] F4/most modern texts = 'reverend', Qq/F1 - 3 = 'reverent'

P/LS [9] though Qq/Ff assign the speech to Marcus, most modern texts assign it to a Roman, sometimes Emillius, sometimes another unnamed Roman Lord

WHO/SD [10] most modern texts indicate this is spoken to Guards or Attendants, who exit at the end of the speech

P [11] most modern texts suggest thus is spoken by all the Romans: Qq/Ff maintain the line as the end of Marcus' speech

525	Lucius	Thankes gentle Romanes, may I governe so,
		To heale Romes harmes, and wipe away her woe.
		But gentle people, give me ayme a-while,
		For Nature puts me to a heavy taske:
		Stand all aloofe, but Unckle draw you neere,
530		To shed obsequious teares upon this Trunke:
		Oh take this warme kisse on thy pale cold lips,
		These sorrowfull drops upon thy bloud-slaine [1] face,
		The last true Duties of thy Noble Sonne.
	Marcus	Teare for teare, and loving kisse for kisse,
535		Thy Brother Marcus tenders on thy Lips:
		O were the summe of these that I should pay
		Countlesse, and infinit, yet would I pay them.
	Lucius	Come hither Boy, come, come, and learne of us
		To melt in showres: thy Grandsire lov'd thee well:
540		Many a time he danc'd thee on his knee:
		Sung thee asleepe, his Loving Brest, thy Pillow:
		Many a matter [2] hath he told to thee,

	[3]	Meete, and agreeing with thine Infancie:
	†[4]	In that respect then, like a loving Childe,
545		Shed yet some small drops from thy tender Spring,
		Because kinde Nature doth require it so:
		Friends, should associate Friends, in Greefe and Wo.
		Bid him farwell, commit him to the Grave,
		Do him that kindnesse, and take leave of him.

550	Boy	O Grandsire, Grandsire: even with all my heart	
		Would I were Dead, so you did Live againe.	
		O Lord, I cannot speake to him for weeping,	
		My teares will choake me, if I ope my mouth.	L 52 - b

W [1] F3/most modern texts = 'bloodstained': Q1 - 2 = 'blood slaine', Q3/F1 - 2 = 'bloud-slaine'

W [2] Q1/most modern texts = 'story', Q2 - 3/Ff = 'matter'

LS [3] most modern texts set an alternative passage from Q1 as follows

And bid thee bare his prettie tales in minde,
And talke of them when he was dead and gone.

Marcus   How many thousand times hath these poore lips,
When they were living warmed themselves on thine,
Oh sweet boy give them their latest kisse,
Bid him farewell commit him to the grave,
Doe them that kindnes and take leave of them.

[4] in F1, the setting of the capital 'I' has risen out of position to hold a peculiar spot halfway between this and the previous line

Romans	1	You sad Andronici, have done with woes,
555		Give sentence on this execrable Wretch,
		That hath beene breeder of these dire events.

Lucius   Set him brest deepe in earth, and famish him:
There let him stand, and rave, and cry for foode:
If any one releeves, or pitties him,
560   For the offence, he dyes.
                            This is our doome:
Some stay, to see him fast'ned in the earth.

Aaron   O [2] why should wrath be mute, & Fury dumbe?
I am no Baby I, that with base Prayers
565   I should repent the Evils I have done.

Ten thousand worse, then ever yet I did,
Would I performe if I might have my will:
If one good Deed in all my life I did,
I do repent if from my very Soule.

570 **Lucius**   Some loving Friends convey the Emp. [3] hence,
And give him buriall in his Fathers grave.

My Father, and Lavinia, shall forthwith
Be closed in our Housholds Monument:
As for that heynous [4] Tyger Tamora,
575   No Funerall Rite, nor man in mournfull Weeds: [5]
No mournfull Bell shall ring her Buriall:
But throw her foorth to Beasts and Birds of [6] prey:
Her life was Beast-like, and devoid of pitty,

7 And being so, shall have like want of pitty.
580   See Justice done on Aaron that damn'd Moore,
From whom, our heavy happes had their beginning:
Then afterwards, to Order well the State,
That like Events, may ne're it Ruinate.

               [Exeunt omnes]   Baby?

R 52 - b : 5. 3. 176 - 200 + last four F1 lines not set

SD 1
    most modern texts indicate that Aaron is now brought in under guard

▼ 2
    Qq/most modern texts = 'Ah', Ff = 'O'

▼ 3
    F1 sets the abbreviation 'Emp.', Qq/F2/most modern texts = 'Emperour'

▼ 4
    Q1/most modern texts = 'ravinous', Q2 - 3/Ff = 'heynous'

▼ 5
    Q1/most modern texts = 'weede', Q2 - 3/Ff = 'Weeds'

▼ 6
    Qq/most modern texts = 'to', Ff = 'of'

COMP/W/LS 7
    again because of the damaged Q1 text used for the setting up of Q2, most modern texts suggest the Q2
compositor was forced to invent part of this first line and, feeling there were lines missing, added five more of
his own: thus most modern texts omit the last four lines as set by Q2 - 3/Ff, and set the Q1 version of this
first line, viz. 'And being dead let birds on her take pittie.'

FINIS

R 52 - b

APPENDIX A
THE UNEASY RELATIONSHIP OF FOLIO,
QUARTOS, AND MODERN TEXTS

Between the years 1590 and 1611, one William Shakespeare, a playwright and actor, delivered to the company of which he was a major shareholder at least thirty-seven plays in handwritten manuscript form. Since the texts belonged to the company upon delivery, he derived no extra income from publishing them. Indeed, as far as scholars can establish, he took no interest in the publication of his plays.

Consequently, without his supervision, yet during his lifetime and shortly after, several different publishers printed eighteen of these plays, each in separate editions. Each of these texts, known as **'Quartos'** because of the page size and method of folding each printed sheet, was about the size of a modern hardback novel. In 1623, seven years after Shakespeare's death, Heminges and Condell, two friends, theatrical colleagues, actors, and fellow shareholders in the company, passed on to the printer, William Jaggard, the handwritten copies of not only these eighteen plays but a further eighteen, of which seventeen had been performed but not yet seen in print.[1] These thirty-six plays were issued in one large volume, each page about the size of a modern legal piece of paper. Anything printed in this larger format was known as 'folio', again because of the page size and the method of sheet folding. Thus the 1623 printing of the collected works is known as **the First Folio**, its 1632 reprint (with more than 1600 unauthorised corrections) the Second Folio, and the next reprint, the 1666 Third Folio, added the one missing play, *Pericles* (which had been set in quarto and performed).

The handwritten manuscript used for the copies of the texts from which both Quartos and the First Folio were printed came from a variety of sources. Closest to Shakespeare were those in his own hand, known as the 'foul papers' because of the natural blottings, crossings out, and corrections. Sometimes he had time to pass the material on to a manuscript copyist who would make a clean copy, known as the 'fair papers'. Whether fair (if there was sufficient time) or foul (if the performance deadline was close), the papers would be passed on to the Playhouse, where a 'Playhouse copy' would be made, from which the 'sides' (individual copies of each part with just a single cue line) would be prepared for each actor. Whether Playhouse copy, fair papers, or foul, the various Elizabethan and Jacobean handwritten manuscripts from which the quartos and Folio came have long since disappeared.

The first printed texts of the Shakespeare plays were products of a speaking-

---

[1] Though written between 1605–09, *Timon of Athens* was not performed publicly until 1761.

hearing society. They were based on rhetoric, a verbal form of arranging logic and argument in a persuasive, pleasing, and entertaining fashion so as to win personal and public debates, a system which allowed individuals to express at one and the same time the steppingstones in an argument while releasing the underlying emotional feelings that accompanied it.[2] Naturally, when ideas were set on paper they mirrored this same form of progression in argument and the accompanying personal release, allowing both neat and untidy thoughts to be seen at a glance (see the General Introduction, pp. xvi–xxi). Thus what was set on paper was not just a silent debate. It was at the same time a reminder of how the human voice might be heard both logically and passionately in that debate.

Such reminders did not last into the eighteenth century. Three separate but interrelated needs insisted on cleaning up the original printings so that silent and speaking reader alike could more easily appreciate the beauties of one of England's greatest geniuses.

First, by 1700, publishing's main thrust was to provide texts to be read privately by people of taste and learning. Since grammar was now the foundation for all writing, publication, and reading, all the Elizabethan and early Jacobean material still based on rhetoric appeared at best archaic and at worst incomprehensible. All printing followed the new universality of grammatical and syntactical standards, standards which still apply today. Consequently any earlier book printed prior to the establishment of these standards had to be reshaped in order to be understood. And the Folio/Quarto scripts, even the revamped versions which had already begun to appear, presented problems in this regard, especially when dealing in the moments of messy human behaviour. Thus, while the first texts were reshaped according to the grammatical knowledge of the 1700s, much of the shaping of the rhetoric was (inadvertently) removed from the plays.

Secondly, the more Shakespeare came to be recognized as a literary poet rather than as a theatrical genius, the less the plays were likely to be considered as performance texts. Indeed plot lines of several of his plays were altered (or ignored) to satisfy the more refined tastes of the period. And the resultant demands for poetic and literary clarity, as well as those of grammar, altered the first printings even further.

Thirdly, scholars argued a need for revision of both Quarto and Folio texts because of 'interfering hands' (hands other than Shakespeare's) having had undue influence on the texts. No matter whether foul or fair papers or Playhouse copy, so the argument ran, several intermediaries would be involved between Shakespeare's writ-

---

[2]   For an extraordinarily full analysis of the art of rhetoric, readers are guided to Sister Miriam Joseph, *Shakespeare's Use of the Arts of Language* (New York: Haffner Publishing Co., 1947). For a more theatrical overview, readers are directed to Bertram Joseph, *Acting Shakespeare* (New York: Theatre Arts Books, 1960). For an overview involving aspects of Ff/Qq, readers are immodestly recommended to Neil Freeman, *Shakespeare's First Texts*, op. cit.

ing of the plays and the printing of them. If the fair papers provided the source text, a copyist might add some peculiarities, as per the well documented Ralph Crane.[3] If the Playhouse copy was the source text, extra information, mainly stage directions, would have been added by someone other than Shakespeare, turning the play from a somewhat literary document into a performance text. Finally, while more than five different compositors were involved in setting the First Folio, five did the bulk of the printing house work: each would have their individual pattern of typesetting — compositor E being singled out as far weaker than the rest. Thus between Shakespeare and the printed text might lie the hand(s) of as few as one and as many as three other people, even more when more than one compositor set an individual play. Therefore critics argue because there is the chance of so much interference between Shakespearean intent and the first printings of the plays, the plays do not offer a stylistic whole, i.e., while the words themselves are less likely to be interfered with, their shapings, the material consistently altered in the early 1700s, are not that of a single hand, and thus cannot be relied upon.

These well-intentioned grammatical and poetic alterations may have introduced Shakespeare to a wider reading audience, but their unforeseen effect was to remove the Elizabethan flavour of argument and of character development (especially in the areas of stress and the resulting textual irregularities), thus watering down and removing literally thousands of rhetorical and theatrical clues that those first performance scripts contained. And it is from this period that the division between ancient and modern texts begins. As a gross generalisation, the first texts, the First Folio and the quartos, could be dubbed 'Shakespeare for the stage'; the second, revamped early 1700 texts 'Shakespeare for the page'.

And virtually all current editions are based on the page texts of the early 1700s. While the words of each play remain basically the same, what shapes them, their sentences, punctuation, spelling, capitalisation, and sometimes even line structure, is often altered, unwittingly destroying much of their practical theatrical value.

It is important to neither condemn the modern editions nor blindly accept the authority of the early stage texts as gospel. This is not a case of 'old texts good, so modern texts bad'. The modern texts are of great help in literary and historical research, especially as to the meanings of obscure words and phrases, and in explaining literary allusions and historical events. They offer guidance to alternative text readings made by reputed editors, plus sound grammatical readings of difficult pas-

---

[3] Though not of the theatre (his principle work was to copy material for lawyers) Crane was involved in the preparation of at least five plays in the Folio, as well as two plays for Thomas Middleton. Scholars characterise his work as demonstrating regular and careful scene and act division, though he is criticised for his heavy use of punctuation and parentheses, apostrophes and hyphens, and 'massed entry' stage directions, i.e. where all the characters with entrances in the scene are listed in a single direction at the top of the scene irrespective of where they are supposed to enter.

sages and clarification of errors that appear in the first printings.[4] In short, they can give the starting point of the play's journey, an understanding of the story, and the conflict between characters within the story. But they can only go so far.

They cannot give you fully the conflict within each character, the very essence for the fullest understanding of the development and resolution of any Shakespeare play. Thanks to their rhetorical, theatrical base the old texts add this vital extra element. They illustrate with great clarity the 'ever-changing present' (see p. xvi in the General Introduction) in the intellectual and emotional life of each character; their passages of harmony and dysfunction, and transitions between such passages; the moments of their personal costs or rewards; and their sensual verbal dance of debate and release. In short, the old texts clearly demonstrate the essential elements of living, breathing, reacting humanity—especially in times of joyous or painful stress.

By presenting the information contained in the First Folio, together with modern restructurings, both tested against theatrical possibilities, these texts should go far in bridging the gap between the two different points of view.

---

[4] For example, the peculiar phrase 'a Table of greene fields' assigned to Mistress Quickly in describing the death of Falstaffe, *Henry V* (Act Two, Scene 3), has been superbly diagnosed as a case of poor penmanship being badly transcribed: the modern texts wisely set 'a babbled of green fields' instead.

NEIL FREEMAN trained as an actor at the Bristol Old Vic Theatre School. He has acted and directed in England, Canada, and the USA. Currently he is an Head of Graduate Directing and Senior Acting Professor in the Professional Training Programme of the Department of Theatre, Film, and Creative Writing at the University of British Columbia. He also teaches regularly at the National Theatre School of Canada, Concordia University, Brigham Young University in both Provo and Hawaii, and is on the teaching faculty of professional workshops in Montreal, Toronto and Vancouver. He is associated with Shakespeare & Co. in Lenox; the Will Geer Theatre in Los Angeles; Bard on the Beach in Vancouver; Repercussion Theatre in Montreal; and has worked with the Stratford Festival, Canada, and Shakespeare Santa Cruz.

His ground breaking work in using the first printings of the Shakespeare texts in performance, on the rehearsal floor and in the classroom has lead to lectures at the Shakespeare Association of America and workshops at both the ATHE and VASTA, and grants/fellowships from the National Endowment of the Arts (USA), The Social Science and Humanities Research Council (Canada), and York University in Toronto.

His three collations of Shakespeare and music - *A Midsummer Nights Dream* (for three actors, chorus, and Orchestra); *If This Be Love* (for three actors, mezzo-soprano, and Orchestra); *The Four Seasons of Shakespeare and Vivaldi* (for two actors, violin soloist and Chamber Orchestra) - commissioned and performed by Bard On The Beach and The Vancouver Symphony Orchestra have been received with great public acclaim.

RECYCLING SHAKESPEARE
by Charles Marowitz

Marowitz' irreverent approach to the bard is
destined to outrage Shakespearean scholars across
the globe. Marowitz rejects the notion that a "classic"
is a sacrosanct entity fixed in time and bounded by its
text. A living classic, according to Marowitz, should
provoke lively response—even indignation!

In the same way that Shakespeare himself
continued to meditate and transform his own ideas
and the shape they took, Marowitz gives us license to
continue that meditation in productions extrapolated
from Shakespeare's work. Shakespeare becomes the
greatest of all catalysts who stimulates a constant re-
formulation of the fundamental questions of
philosophy, history and meaning. Marowitz
introduces us to Shakespeare as an active
contemporary collaborator who strives with us to
yield a vibrant contemporary theatre.

paper • ISBN: 1-55783-094-0

SHAKESPEARE'S PLAYS IN PERFORMANCE
by John Russell Brown

In this volume, John Russell Brown snatches Shakespeare from the clutches of dusty academics and thrusts him centerstage where he belongs—in performance.

Brown's thorough analysis of the theatrical experience of Shakespeare forcibly demonstrates how the text is brought to life: awakened, colored, emphasized, and extended by actors and audiences, designers and directors.

"A knowledge of what precisely can and should happen when a play is performed is, for me, the essential first step towards an understanding of Shakespeare."
—from the Introduction by John Russell Brown

paper•ISBN 1-55783-136-X•

 **APPLAUSE**

SHAKESCENES:
SHAKESPEARE
FOR TWO
The Shakespeare Scenebook

EDITED AND WITH AN INTRODUCTION
BY JOHN RUSSELL BROWN

Shakespeare's plays are not the preserve of
"Shakespearean Actors" who specialize in a
remote species of dramatic life. Shakespeare asks to
be performed by all good actors. Here in the
introduction, "Advice to Actors," and in the notes to
each of thirty–five scenes, John Russell Brown offers
sensible guidance for those who have little or no
experience with the formidable Bard. Thirty-five
scenes are presented in newly edited texts, with notes
which clarify meanings, topical references, puns,
ambiguities, etc. Each scene has been chosen for its
independent life requiring only the simplest of stage
properties and the barest of spaces. A brief
description of characters and situation prefaces each
scene and is followed by a commentary which
discusses its major acting challenges and
opportunities.

paper • ISBN 1-55783-049-5

THE APPLAUSE
SHAKESPEARE LIBRARY
General Editor: John Russell Brown

"The Applause Shakespeare is a pioneering edition, responding to an old challenge in a new way and trying to break down barriers to understanding that have proved very obstinate for a long time."
— John Russell Brown

These new Applause editions allow the reader to look beyond the scholarly text to the more collaborative and malleable *performance* text — each note, each gloss, each commentary reflects the stage life of the play.

Available Now:

Macbeth
$7.95 • PAPER • ISBN 1-55783-180-7

A Midsummer Night's Dream
$7.95 • PAPER • ISBN 1-55783-181-5

King Lear
$7.95 • PAPER • ISBN 1-55783-179-3

The Tempest
$7.95 • PAPER • ISBN 1-55783-182-3

Julius Caesar
$7.95 • PAPER • ISBN 1-55783-183-1

 APPLAUSE

MEDIEVAL AND TUDOR DRAMA
Twenty-four Plays
Edited and with introductions
by John Gassner

The rich tapestry of medieval belief, morality and
manners shines through this comprehensive
anthology of the twenty-four major plays that bridge
the dramatic worlds of medieval and Tudor England.
Here are the plays that paved the way to the
Renaissance and Shakespeare. In John Gassner's
extensively annotated collection, the plays regain
their timeless appeal and display their truly
international character and influence.

Medieval and Tudor Drama remains the
indispensable chronicle of a dramatic heritage — the
classical plays of Hrotsvitha, folk and ritual drama,
the passion play, the great morality play *Everyman*,
the Interlude, Tudor comedies *Ralph Roister Doister*
and *Gammer Gurton's Needle*, and the most famous of
Tudor tragedies *Gorboduc*. The texts have been
modernized for today's readers and those composed
in Latin have been translated into English.

paper • ISBN: 0-936839-84-8

THE REDUCED SHAKESPEARE COMPANY'S
COMPLEAT WORKS OF WLLM SHKSPR
(abridged)
by JESS BORGESON, ADAM LONG, and DANIEL SINGER

"ABSL HLRS." —*The Independent* (London)

"Shakespeare writ small, as you might like it! . . . Pithier-than-Python parodies . . . not to be confused with that august English company with the same initials. This iconoclastic American Troupe does more with less."

> — *The New York Times*

"Shakespeare as written by *Reader's Digest*, acted by Monty Python, and performed at the speed of the Minute Waltz. So Forsooth! Get thee to the RSC's delightfully fractured *Compleat Works*."

> — *Los Angeles Herald*

ISBN 1-55783-157-2 • $8.95 • PAPER

SOLILOQUY!

The Shakespeare Monologues
Edited by Michael Earley and Philippa Keil

At last, over 175 of Shakespeare's finest and most performable monologues taken from all 37 plays are here in two easy-to-use volumes (MEN and WOMEN). Selections travel the entire spectrum of the great dramatist's vision, from comedies and romances to tragedies, pathos and histories.

"*Soliloquy is an excellent and comprehensive collection of Shakespeare's speeches. Not only are the monologues wide-ranging and varied, but they are superbly annotated. Each volume is prefaced by an informative and reassuring introduction, which explains the signals and signposts by which Shakespeare helps an actor on his journey through the text. It includes a very good explanation of blank verse, with excellent examples of irregularities which are specifically related to character and acting intentions. These two books are a must for any actor in search of a 'classical' audition piece.*"

ELIZABETH SMITH
Head of Voice & Speech
The Juilliard School

paper—MEN: ISBN 0-936839-78-3
WOMEN: ISBN 0-936839-79-1

THE ACTOR AND THE TEXT
by Cicely Berry

As voice director of the Royal Shakespeare Company, Cicely Berry has worked with actors such as Jeremy Irons, Derek Jacobi, Jonathan Pryce, Sinead Cusack and Antony Sher. *The Actor and The Text* brings Ms. Berry's methods of applying vocal production skills within a text to the general public.

While this book focuses primarily on speaking Shakespeare, Ms. Berry also includes the speaking of some modern playwrights, such as Edward Bond.

As Ms. Berry describes her own volume in the introduction:

" ... this book is not simply about making the voice sound more interesting. It is about getting inside the words we use ...It is about making the language organic, so that the words act as a spur to the sound ..."

paper•ISBN 1–155783–138–6

SHAKESPEARE'S FIRST TEXTS
by Neil Freeman

"THE ACTOR'S BEST CHAMPION OF THE
FOLIO"   —Kristin Linklater
author of *Freeing Shakespeare's Voice*

Neil Freeman provides students, scholars, theatre-lovers, and, most importantly, actors and directors, with a highly readable, illuminating, and indispensable guide to William Shakespeare's own first quill-inscribed texts — SHAKESPEARE'S FIRST TEXTS.

Four hundred years later, most of the grammatical and typographical information conveyed by this representation in Elizabethan type by the first play compositors has been lost. Or, rather, discarded, in order to conform to the new standards of usage. Granted, this permitted more readers access to Shakespeare's writing, but it also did away with some of Shakespeare himself.

ISBN 1-155783-335-4